# Social Media Marketing

# Social Media Marketing

## Marketing Panacea or the Emperor's New Digital Clothes?

Alan Charlesworth

BEP BUSINESS EXPERT PRESS

First published in 2018 by
Business Expert Press, LLC
222 East 46th Street, New York, NY 10017
www.businessexpertpress.com

ISBN-13: 978-1-63157-764-2 (paperback)
ISBN-13: 978-1-63157-765-9 (e-book)

Business Expert Press Marketing Strategy Collection

Collection ISSN: 2150-9654 (print)
Collection ISSN: 2150-9662 (electronic)

Cover and interior design by Exeter Premedia Services Private Ltd., Chennai, India

First edition: 2018

10 9 8 7 6 5 4 3 2 1

Printed in the United States of America.

*Not Doctor. Not Professor. Just Mister.*

# Abstract

The tale of The Emperor's New Clothes cautions people about accepting whatever so-called experts tell us without question. In this book, Hans Christian Andersen's cautionary anecdote provides the backdrop to a comprehensive review of the use of social media platforms in the marketing of an organization, brand, or product.

Chapter one provides the reader with a background to social media. This starts with its history and adoption in the digital age before going on to identify the key elements that make up digital social media, namely, social networks, online communities, social sharing, user-generated content, and blogging.

The introductory nature of the content continues in chapter two where the public's use of social media is examined along with the digital platforms on which it is conducted. The chapter concludes with a consideration of why the public might interact with organizations, brands, or products on social media.

Chapter three provides an analysis of what social media marketing consists and what it does not. Details of the key models associated with social media marketing are also included.

In chapter four, an organization's strategic expectations of marketing on social media are addressed, as are how its success, or otherwise, can be measured and issues related to any potential return on investment. The chapter concludes with an evaluation of the role that the culture of any organization, brand, or product plays in effective social media marketing.

Chapter five deliberates the operational aspects of marketing on social media from its management through which employees actually do what, and when they do it. Also reflected upon is the use of third party platforms by social media marketers.

The key feature of chapter six is analysis of examples of social media marketing in practice, allowing conclusions to be made on what works, what doesn't, and why.

As might be expected in a conclusion, chapter seven brings together the issues raised in previous chapters, throws in a few new ideas, and encourages readers to draw their own conclusion on whether marketing on social media is indeed a marketing panacea or the Emperor's New Digital Clothes.

# Keywords

digital marketing, digital transformation, e-commerce, Internet marketing, marketing on social media, online marketing, social media advertising, social media marketing, social media, viral marketing

# Contents

# Preface

Throughout the book it is necessary to give examples of the various platforms being covered within the chapters. In this regard I have taken the easy path of using those platforms and brands that are most popular at the time the book went to press, namely the likes of Facebook, YouTube, Instagram, and Twitter. However, my reason for this is that the majority of readers will recognize them, and it should not be perceived as *favoritism* on my part. Indeed, these branded social media platforms do not carry all before them in other parts of the world. For example, there is Orkut in Brazil, VKontakte and Odnoklassniki in Russia, Cyword and Me2day in South Korea, and Qzone, Tencent Weibo, and Sina Weibo in China.

When talking about social media presences I constantly refer to *products*, *brands*, and *organizations*. My reasoning for this is that such is the nature of social media that—for example—a Facebook page could be a marketing tool for a product, a brand, or an organization, where the content is written on behalf of that product, brand, or organization. In the case of *organizations* these can be not-for-profit or public body as well as a company or firm.

Scattered throughout the book are references to organizations with which I have worked—be that as a consultant or as part of my research—but none are named. In these examples, the identity of the organization would not add to the readers' understanding of the subject and so I choose to not make public my association with them—or theirs with me—or because I have signed a confidentiality agreement which means they have to remain anonymous whether I like it or not. In other examples—particularly in Chapter 6—stories are available online for everyone to see, and so no anonymity is necessary. It is also the case in these illustrations that the nature of the organization, brand, or product is pertinent to the point I am making.

There are a number of occasions in the book where I refer readers to a website, or even advise a case is sought on a search engine rather than include full details within the text. I also, on occasion, type out messages posted on social media platforms rather than presenting them verbatim as a cut-copy-paste image. I would prefer to use an image of a website, tweet, or Facebook page. However, the organizations concerned either refuse outright requests for permission to reproduce those images, or make the process so laborious it—effectively—puts authors and/or publishers off of the idea.[1]

Such is the fast-moving nature of both social media and any marketing conducted on that media, I feel it is worth pointing out that the bulk of this book was written in winter/spring of 2017. So if you think any of the content looks a bit dated by the time you read, please bear in mind that the process of publishing a book is not instantaneous. Thank you.

---

[1] I have written about this issue before; if you have an interest take a look at its web page—it's an academic paper, so a bit long-winded, but you can always skip to the interesting bits in the chart at the end. See alancharlesworth.eu/free-publicity-you-cant-give-it-away/index.html.

# Acknowledgments

All the students, trainees, and audiences at any event at which I have spoken—if you hadn't asked the questions, I would not have had to find the answers.

All those practitioners, writers, bloggers, and researchers who do the work that keeps people like me informed.

All those organizations that have asked me to monitor or participate in their digital marketing efforts—you learn more in an hour at the sharp end than you do in weeks of reading the theory.

Those colleagues who have supported and encouraged me in writing this, and other books. It is a constant grievance of mine that academia values papers read by only a few over textbooks that help educate thousands.

All those at Business Expert Press who helped make this book happen.

To the Exeter team for converting my British-English manuscript to American-English and adapting it to the house style of BEP—both of which are rather alien to me. If there's anything *British* still in that's because I insisted on it.

And finally Rudyard Kipling for the quotes at the beginning of each chapter. Now there's a man who could tell a yarn.

# Introduction

*There is no sin so great as ignorance. Remember this.*

According to the first line of their website, "Inc. 5000 are the superheroes of the U.S. economy. America's fastest-growing private companies wield powers like strategy, service, and innovation."

These superheroes are the newcomers to business and so, by definition, newcomers to marketing. Their example—surely—must represent the future of *effective* marketing. And that marketing future *must* lie in the arms of social media. Why? Because *everyone* says so. Well nearly everyone. Some people are standing up in the crowd and suggesting that we are all being told how handsome the Emperor looks in his new clothes.

Research by Barnes and Daubitz (2017) highlighted the methods of marketing favored by the Inc. 5000 companies, in particular their choice of channels to increase sales by asking the question "which of the following do you feel provides the most potential for increasing sales for your company in the next 12 months?" In Barnes and Daubitz' research, the options included blogging and social media platforms LinkedIn, Facebook, Twitter, Instagram, YouTube, Google Plus, and Pinterest. The results were as follows: social networking platforms 41 percent; online advertising 21 percent; traditional print/broadcast media 9 percent; business directory listings 6 percent; daily deal sites 2 percent; others 19 percent. Not quite a clean sweep for social media—but with it representing not far off half of all efforts in increasing sales, it's a clear winner. That's some suit of clothes for the Emperor.

The key highlights of the report also identified that 94 percent of the Inc. 5000 companies have a LinkedIn account, 88 percent have a Facebook account, and 79 percent have a Twitter account. Those new clothes are looking finer by the minute.

However, further into the report's findings some folks might raise an eyebrow when respondents identify that the top benefit of social media marketing is building brand awareness. *Excuse me?* say some as they reach for their spectacles for a better look at the Emperor; you're saying that social media is your top choice for increasing sales—but you think that social media is best for building brand awareness. Since when did brand awareness guarantee an increase in sales? Perhaps for these *superheroes* traditional marketing theory and practice don't apply?

But it is when the researchers posed a question with regard to the *superheroes'* main concerns about the use of social media as their primary source of new customers that binoculars should have been handed out to seek out a closer look at the Emperor's clothes. Those concerns were: the return on investment, time allocation, and resources devoted to social media. I wonder how many of these executives would commit themselves so wholeheartedly to *any* other aspect of their business whilst doubting not only the return on any investment, but being unsure of the demands on staff and resources. I would suggest that the answer to that question is *none*.

Could it be that these executives have been taken in by the Emperor's New *Digital* Clothes?

# CHAPTER 1

# What Is Social Media

*Words are, of course, the most powerful drug used by mankind*

## 1.1 Introduction

The generation that has grown up with the Internet has also grown up with the assumption that social media is a creation of their generation. But they are wrong. Tom Standage, in his influential 2013 book *Writing on the Wall*, tells us that social media can be traced back over 2,000 years. In Roman times members of the elite in society would not only exchange letters with individuals, but encourage that the content of those letters be copied and shared with fellow members of their social circles. Such sharing was normally via speeches and books—but these messages were also posted on the walls of buildings in public areas. Note how the term for placing a message on a publicly viewable space is called *posting*. As in: we *post* messages. As in: *posting* a message on social media. Mr Zuckerberg et al didn't invent a new term for the act when they developed Facebook; they used a good old English term (actually, its etymology is Latin, but you get my drift). I mention this because, whilst the technology has changed since those times, the need to connect with friends and members of the community to share information remains as we progress through the 21st century. Standage goes on to assert that many of the issues—both positive and negative—raised by *digital* social media have arisen before and so history might provide some valuable lessons to the contemporary digital marketer.

Long before Internet technology made it possible, social contact existed between communities of like-minded people who shared views on anything from sports teams through politics to the best way to prune roses. Importantly, however, such communication was restricted by the logistics of geography and the limitations of communication tools available to those generations. Effectively, your social contact existed only between a close circle of friends and associates. For the marketer, this limited the number of people to whom you could express delight or criticism of a product, brand, or organization. Such restrictions do not exist for the digital generation. Be it on a PC, laptop, or handheld device, user-generated content can be diffused around the globe at the click of a mouse or—as is now most common—the touch of a screen.

## 1.2 So What Is *Digital* Social Media?

Such is the nature of the subject that it is possible—even likely—that any definition offered on these pages might be out-of-date before they are published. This is, perhaps, an exaggeration, but when a previous book of mine (*An Introduction to Social Media Marketing*) was published in 2015 the content included no mention of *Periscope* because it simply did not exist when the book was written. Not only that, in little over a year, *Periscope* was launched, bought by Twitter and relaunched. Furthermore, in December 2016 Twitter announced the launch of *Twitter Live*, which—as it's essentially the same—may turn out to be a replacement for Periscope. *Vine*, on the other hand, was included in *An Introduction to Social Media Marketing*, but it pretty much ceased to exist in 2016 (at the time of writing, owners Twitter had announced its relegation to being a limited-application camera app).

Although any definition might be fleeting, a book on social media *marketing* must at least make some attempt to offer a definition of what social media is. In another book from way back in the first decade of the century (time moves very fast in digital circles), I defined social media as: "a collective term for the various social network and community sites including such online applications as blogs, podcasts, reviews and wikis" (Charlesworth 2009). At the time I deliberated over replacing *collective* with *umbrella*. In retrospect, I think I prefer the latter. These days I tend to use a rather vague, though perhaps more tangible, definition of: "any web presence where users can add their own content but do not have control over the site in the same way as they would their own website" (Charlesworth 2014). These definitions reveal a conviction on my part that (a) social media existed long before the digital revolution made it a cultural phenomenon, and (b) social media is not social media if the content is published on the writer's own website. A caveat to this is that it is an indication of the uncertainty as to what social media actually is that even the author of books on social media can confuse the issue. Sharp-eyed readers will notice that later in this tome I list *blogging* as being an aspect of social media, and yet it is not unusual for a blog to appear on its author's own website and/or domain name.

At this point it would be sensible to offer the reader other pertinent definitions—and I will, once another issue is addressed. In the previous paragraph I treated *social media* as a noun, but it might also be considered that in the term social media, *media* is a noun and *social* is its adjective. I'll stick with it being a noun, but as has become in the case with the word *data*, a noun that can be used as singular or plural without English scholars getting too upset. I doubt you will have seen Facebook described as social medium, or as I say in this book social media *is*, not social media *are*. Ho hum, let's move on and hope that sometime in the future historians can write: "eventually the digital people got their act together and came up with a definition for social media with which everyone agreed."

I'll end this section by throwing another spanner into the metaphorical definition works. The definitions presented refer to websites—but websites could just as easily be replaced with *tools*. Or when social media is conducted on mobile devices, *apps*. And in a class yesterday I found myself using the term *platforms* to describe Facebook, Twitter, Instagram, et al. So I looked up the *technical* meaning of the word and got this from *techopedia.com:* "A platform is a group of technologies that are used as a base upon which other applications, processes or technologies are developed." In personal computing, a platform is the basic hardware (computer) and software (operating system) on which software applications can be run. From my less-than-technical point of view isn't that everything on a computer? However, referring to platforms has a sensible ring to it—and I can even elicit the support of Mark Zuckerberg on this as he has described Facebook as a platform.[1]

---

[1] In a live interview with Sheryl Sandberg in December 2016. Available on: https://www.facebook.com/zuck/videos/10103353645165001/

So what other definitions of *social media* are out there? Two from old school dictionaries are: "forms of electronic communication (such as Web sites) through which people create online communities to share information, ideas, personal messages, etc;" (Merriam-Webster) and "websites and applications that enable users to create and share content or to participate in social networking" (Oxford Dictionaries). These are similar, with an emphasis on networking and communities. Cambridge University Press offer up: "websites and computer programs that allow people to communicate and share information on the internet using a computer or mobile phone." This definition seems a bit, well: loose. "Computer programs?" In this context, isn't that software? Or do they mean apps? And "communicate and share." Does that mean communicate *in order to* share or communicate *as well as* share? Or both? But their example of the term used in a sentence then takes us on a tangent to the definition by saying: "companies are increasingly making use of social media in order to market their goods." I'll come on to social media marketing in Chapter 3, but it is generally accepted that social media is, was, and always will be, for *people* to "communicate and share information." That organizations have hijacked it to carry marketing messages should not take us away from the original concept.

Dictionary.com also uses a business example rather than a social one in its sample sentence ("many businesses are utilizing social media to generate sales") after its more societal definition of: "websites and other online means of communication that are used by large groups of people to share information and to develop social and professional contacts." If I was to be picky on this one, I ask what "large" is in this context.

Moving away from traditional sources into the digital arena, that doyen of crowd-sourced information, Wikipedia states that: "Social media are computer-mediated technologies that allow the creating and sharing of information, ideas, career interests and other forms of expression via virtual communities and networks." However, it follows the theme of this chapter by adding: The variety of stand-alone and built-in social media services currently available introduces challenges of definition. Techopedia (techopedia.com) is far more helpful for the purposes of this book, not least by offering examples, when it says:

Social media is a catch-all term for a variety of Internet applications that allow users to create content and interact with each other. This interaction can take many forms, but some common types include:

- Sharing links to interesting content produced by third parties
- Public updates to a profile, including information on current activities and even location data
- Sharing photos, videos, and posts
- Commenting on the photos, posts, updates, videos, etc. shared by others.

Worth noting is that the first in this list describes the original use of the term blog, where—in the days before search engines—surfers would seek out lists of websites that had been compiled by bloggers. Not unlike the nature of many contemporary blogs, these bloggers were showing off to newbie surfers by saying: "check me out, I've been to all these sites before you." Kaplan and Haenlein (2010) further associate social media with digital technology when they describe social media as: "a group of Internet-based applications that build on the ideological and technological foundations of Web 2.0 and that allow the creation and exchange of user generated content."

This requires us to consider yet another misunderstood—and misused—term from the digital lexicon, Web 2.0. Kaplan and Haenlein were not the first to make this connection, however. In their influential 2006 book *Wikinomics*, Tapscott and Williams drew popular attention to a link between Web 2.0 and the new social media by suggesting that the *old web* was about websites, clicks, and eyeballs, but the *new web*—Web 2.0—was about the communities and participation. Constantinides and Fountain (2008) followed this up with a paper that gave a definition of Web 2.0 which might also be used to describe social media. They said that: "Web 2.0 applications support the creation of informal users' networks facilitating the flow of ideas and knowledge by allowing the efficient generation, dissemination, sharing and editing/refining of informational content." They went on to identify that social media had potential for business, however, in that it presented businesses "new opportunities for getting and staying in touch with their markets, learning about the needs and opinions of their customers as well as interacting with them in a direct and personalised way."

Based on David Bowen's original concept (entitled Web 2007), Table 1.1 shows the four levels of content on the web that will help readers understand the concept of Web 2.0 as well as demonstrating its link with social media. The matrix attempts to describe how Web 2.0 translates into online activity. The crossover to social media in the four quadrants shows how web content moves from that controlled by the organization through to that over which it has no control (Charlesworth 2014).

McConnell and Huba (2007) suggest that social media is not about the technology, but instead: "the sum total of people who create content online, as well as the people who interact with it or one another." A different slant is offered by Bryan Eisenberg (2008) who puts forward the notion that the various elements that make up social media do not actually represent media but: "a platform for interaction and networking,"

*Table 1.1 The four levels of content on the web*

| | HOME WEB 2 | EXTENDED WEB 2 |
|---|---|---|
| Two-way (horizontal web) | In this square communication is two-way from the organization to the customers—but is controlled by the organization. It is made up of the organization's own blogs and forums. | Elements of this square are those most often associated with Web 2.0. These are the sites over which organizations have no control and people talk to one another. It includes individual's blogs, social network sites, traditional forums or discussion areas, Q & A pages, and sites such as Wikipedia. |
| | **HOME WEB 1** | **EXTENDED WEB 2** |
| One-way (vertical web) | In this quadrant, communication is one-way from the organization, mirroring traditional marketing where the marketing message is controllable. The organization's own website(s), including images, videos, podcasts as well as textual content, makes up this section. | This square represents the websites on which the organization can place content, but they do not control. This includes consumer and review sites as well as (for example) videos on YouTube, photos on Instagram, and groups the organization has set up or sponsored on social network sites such as Facebook. It also includes ads hosted on other sites. |
| | You control (home web) | Others control (extended web) |

*Source:* Charlesworth (2014) from an original idea by David Bowen.

which raises the issue of whether we are trying to define the *publisher* of the communication or the *content* of that communication?

And finally in this roundup of definitions, my sister's description of social media is: "the most dangerous thing in the world." She has a point … but it is an argument for a book on sociology and not marketing.

As is accepted practice in academic publications, I need to determine the definition of social media that is to be used within the content. For this, I'm going back to my definition quoted at the beginning of the chapter as the basis for the definition of social media for the purposes of this book, and that is: an umbrella term for the various social network and community sites that are composed of user-generated content. Sharp-eyed readers will realize that I have replaced *collective* with *umbrella* as I previously suggested. The *user-generated* reference emphasizes that social media is developed by society, as opposed to social media *marketing* where the content is developed by representatives of an organization, brand, or product. This definition is expanded upon in the next two chapters where the various elements of social media are identified when associated with first users and then marketers. However, having declared a definition, it is reasonable to suggest that social media is actually whatever it is perceived to be by any individual participating in it.

So having defined what social media is, what are its constituent parts? Like its definition, the elements of social media are open to debate, but here's my list. However, before that there's something else to clarify. Facebook is not part of social media; it is an entity that exists to facilitate social media. Ditto Twitter. Ditto Instagram. Ditto Snapchat. Ditto any social media brand or platform. Although they are sometimes referred to as social media *tools*, a better term for those organizations that provide access to social media is the aforementioned *platforms*. In years gone by *websites* would have been an adequate description for Facebook et al., but in the days of mobile devices and apps, *platform* fits the bill better, even though some hard-line computer scientists might berate a simple marketer on this assertion (if I was writing this on a social media plat-form and not an academic text, I'd have ended the sentence with a smiley face emoji). Social media platforms can be categorized as either: social networks and online communities, social sharing, blogging, or user gen-erated content. There are, however, a couple of caveats: (a) there are gray areas where these meld together, and (b) remember these are related to *social* activities, not *marketing*—which comes in Chapter 3. It is necessary to emphasize some important and fundamental points with regard to the brand-name platforms: (1) They exist to make money for their owners or shareholders, (2) they do not exist to further mankind's communication, and (3) they do not exist to make marketers' lives easier—though doing so attracts more advertisers, which in turn increases their income, and so pleases their owners and shareholders. We will return to these issues throughout the book.

## 1.3 Social Networks and Online Communities

I find it difficult to differentiate between *social networks* and *online communities*. In his excellent *Marketing to the Social Web*, Larry Weber (2007) seems to have the same problem, stating that social networks are "member-based communities that enable users to link to one another based on common interests and through invites," whilst e-communities are "online sites where people aggregate around a common interest area with topical interest and often includes professional content." The only difference seems to be the issue of professional content on community sites—which is a point well made, but it ignores the fact that sites like YouTube thrive on clips from TV shows and videos of recognized music artists, all of which are very professional.

Looking back to my own definitions from around the same time, in *Key Concepts in e-Commerce* (2007) I mention a term popular at that time but that has fallen out of fashion of late, and that is *virtual*. I refer to the phrase *virtual communities*—attributed to Howard Rheingold, the author and founding executive editor of *Hotwired*—which refers to the way in which people can interact with each other using information technologies rather than face-to-face contact. It is also a sign of the times that back then I also refer to virtual community *websites*, which reflects the era before social media *platforms* or *apps*. In that book I also make an attempt at differentiating *social networks* and *online communities* by stating that all social media sites require content to maintain visitors' interest—and that they soon lose any appeal they may have if that criterion is not met. However, it is perceived usefulness of that content that is a significant antecedent of a member's sense of belonging to the virtual community. This might be an example of how social networking and online communities differ. Facebook, for example, is perceived more as a method of communicating (networking) with friends, be they *virtual* friends or the real-life versions. Communities, on the other hand, are a more select group of people who share an interest, but are not necessarily friends in the traditional sense—with any perceived usefulness of the community extending beyond bonding and togetherness.

## 1.4 Social Sharing

Defining social sharing is problematic. Indeed, although I use Twitter as the mainstay example of social sharing, it would be a reasonable argument for it being in the previous section. Moreover, such are the changes at Facebook—and the way it is used—that some of its functions *might* also be described as sharing. However, let's stick with the definitions of sharing being more of a one-way communication, whereas networking—from the verb, to network—is about making contacts and exchanging ideas, thoughts, and so on. Hence, the likes of YouTube, Instagram, and Snapchat fall into this category. Social sharing is commonly described as the *broadcasting of our thoughts and activities,* which suits the concept of Twitter's $140^2$-character message format, Instagram's service that enables its users to take pictures and videos and send them to friends or the public, and Snapchat's shared images that are both short-lived and self-deleting. That YouTube's content includes—among other things—distinct marketing messages (e.g., TV adverts and public relations events), clips from TV shows and movies, and music videos should not distract us from the raison d'etre for YouTube's social content is video clips posted by the general public, for example, the ubiquitous skateboarding dogs, cuddly cats, and a series of young men performing stunts that result in their personal pain.

---

[2] Whilst the book was in the final stages of publication Twitter confirmed a long-standing rumor that it was raising the character limit from 140 to 280. However, the change was not universally lauded—might it have changed back by the time you read this?

## 1.5 User Generated Content

That we have not yet reached the end of the first chapter and I'm once again introducing a caveat that suggests that the chapter's titular subject is *so* open to interpretation on *so* many levels that perhaps I should start each section with: *in my opinion*—or would that be just a way of covering my back?[3] Like other topics covered in this book, user generated content (UGC) is yet to be bestowed with a definition that is agreeable to everyone. Furthermore, other popular terminology used in the same context as UGC is user generated *media* (UGM) and both of these with the word *user* replaced by *consumer*, that is; consumer generated content (CGC) and consumer generated media (CGM). To add to the confusion, consumer is commonly replaced by *customer*. That customers and consumers are not the same is irrelevant in this context—let's just be glad they start with the same letter and so reduce the range of acronyms. We could get pedantic and examine any possible differentiation of these terms, but in reality there is little—with their application being down to individual preference or practice. Therefore, for the purposes of this book, UGC it is. Although UGC was initially limited to textual content, the popularity of smartphones that come complete with high-quality video and still cameras has served to increase the use of video clips and photographs as UGC. The bulk of UGC that is not considered part of the categories covered in previous sections of this chapter (i.e., social networks and online communities, social sharing, or blogging) is produced as part of reviews and ratings of products or services—hence the use of consumer/customer in CGC.

Note that the subsequent chapters of this book concentrate on how marketers can utilize social media platforms as a channel for their marketing efforts and within that remit marketers can influence online reviews and ratings (e.g., by making them available to potential customers), but genuine UGC has had a significant impact on marketers and marketing as part of social media. A Facebook entry or Tweet praising or condemning a product the writer has used, for example, is merely the passing on of an opinion to friends—and not posting a review for total strangers

---

[3] Another smiley face here, perhaps one with its tongue out on one side of its mouth?

who may be anywhere in the world, to read. Rating sites and/or facilities differ slightly from reviews in that they offer the appraiser a simpler—quicker—alternative to typing out their own review. This can be as easy as clicking on an image of a thumb up or down to signify recommend or not, an overall star rating or more complex multi-element star ratings based on various aspects of the product.

## 1.6 Blogging

Although the term *weblog* was first used in 1997, with *blog* being introduced in 1999, the practice dates back to the early 1990s when individuals who surfed the web and listed (or *logged*) websites that they found interesting, often with their own review of the sites (Charlesworth 2007). Such logged lists—normally in categories—were the way in which folk found websites in the years before search engines existed. One definition of blog that gives an insight into *bloggers* comes from Webopedia[4] which says a blog is: "a web page that serves as a publicly accessible personal journal for an individual. Typically updated daily, blogs often reflect the personality of the author." The last six words of this definition are the key to blogging. Bloggers have attitude. They have an opinion on everything—or a specific subject—and they are not shy about letting others know their views. The best social media writers have similar attributes. For the next 10 years, online blogs developed to the point where they were mini websites based around the thoughts or interests of the writer. Then blog-hosting sites (e.g., blogger.com) which facilitated their easy development became freely available, and the practice of individual blogging increased out of all proportion to what had gone before. That rapid expansion turned into an equally swift decline as a proliferation of alternative platforms of social media resulted in blogging becoming less popular. It is fair to suggest that many personal Facebook pages and Twitter feeds are much the same as the personal blogs that went before them.

It is apt that the chapter ends with an emphasis on the social—personal—aspect of social media. From this point on, the focus of the book is on the commercial use of social media as a marketing tool.

---

[4] www.webopedia.com

# CHAPTER 2

# Who Uses What on Social Media... and Why

*Good Lord! who can account for the fathomless folly of the public?*

## 2.1 Users and User Behavior

### Why People Use Social Media

Social media was not an invention of the digital age—so it is no surprise that the psychological and sociological concept on which effective social media is founded—social exchange theory—also predates the Internet. Indeed, the seminal works on the subject were published by Homans in 1958 and 1961, Thibaut et al. in 1959, and Blau in 1964. Social exchange theory is built on the premise that social behavior results from an exchange process where each party seeks to maximize benefits and minimize costs. Such costs and benefits are not only intangible but differ from individual to individual. Each person weighs cost versus benefit to assess if the exchange is of benefit to them. The theory concludes that if the perceived risks outweigh the potential rewards then any potential relationship will cease. In the real world, not only can the risks and rewards be complex, but the start or end of a relationship can also be fraught with problems. Online, however, they can be more easily gained or discarded—the click of a mouse or tap of a screen being all that is required to accept or reject any social contact. For social media to be effective, however, messages must pass from more than one individual to another—there must be a network of acquaintances to pass them on to.

In his influential paper on social networking, The Strength of Weak Ties (1973), Granovetter takes this a stage further by arguing that acquaintances do not all carry equal rank. We have *strong ties* with family, close friends, and immediate coworkers, those being the most receptive to any contact we make. Those close friends have their own collection of strong ties, but the connection between the two clusters being only a *weak tie*. For any social network to be effective, participants are dependent on both strong and weak relationships (ties) in order for their message to get maximum exposure. Offline, this effectiveness is problematic, being reliant on acquaintances (weak ties) relaying a message to *their* close friends (strong ties) to continue the transmission of a message. In an online environment, however, with the simple click of a mouse, tap of a screen, or voice command, any message can be instantaneously sent to both friends and acquaintances—strong and weak ties. Furthermore, with similar *digital* ease, those people can forward the message to *their* friends and acquaintances (and so on and so on). Geography and time zones present no barrier. Compare that with the Romans writing a message on a wall.

Frenzen and Nakamoto (1993) took the model a stage further by investigating the impact of any benefits (the value of information) and cost (moral hazard) in forwarding the message. In their study, news of a discounted price offer was included in a message—so introducing a business-related element to what was previously a noncommercial concept. In their study, the value—benefit—was the discount rate and the moral aspect—cost—was availability of stock. Any observer of human behavior will not be surprised to learn that as the discount rate rose and the subsequent availability of stock decreased, respondents were far less likely to pass on the message to a wider circle of contacts (their weak links). This was because they perceived that if more people (the weak links) knew the information, then their close friends (strong links) were less likely to benefit. Although their research focused on the *social* aspect of social media, the findings of Cebrian et al. (2017) support the notion that social media isn't totally altruistic, with their team creating a viral campaign that outperformed those of competitors by offering an incentive scheme that motivated people to recruit their social media friends. Although centered on societal issues, Frenzen and Nakamoto's study is also relevant to marketers in their goal of having consumers forward marketing messages to their friends and acquaintances. In Rogers' *Diffusion of Innovations* (1962), for the diffusion to be effective there is a dependence on innovators to pass on their opinion of a product to early adopters, them on to early majority, and so on. At each stage the message-passer will seek to gain kudos from their knowledge (the benefit), but the innovator will want the message to be restricted to close contacts, their status diminishing if the message leaps from innovator to laggard too quickly. Granovetter's *Weak Ties* concept was the basis for a pictorial representation of how relationships with, or connections to, other people spread out from an individual. Called the *Social Graph* the model became fashionable in 2007 when Facebook founder, Mark Zuckerberg, used the phrase to describe his new company's platform. The graph (see Figure 2.1) shows how ties get weaker as they spread from the center. Depending on the strength of their connection these can be described as direct and indirect relationships.

Facebook extended this when in 2010 it launched *Open Graph*—a kind of global chart that had the goal of mapping everybody and how they're related. Although this was of significant interest in social science, it was Facebook's commercial application that piqued the interest of marketers. Open Graph facilitated Facebook in gaining insights into its members and users that could help it sell more advertising—essential for a company with no other source of income. The paradigm was that if someone *liked* a comment made on a Facebook page about—for example—a particular rock band, then it would be a reasonable assumption that the

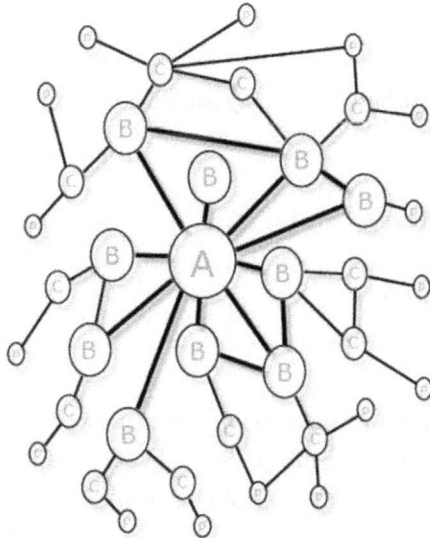

*Figure 2.1 The social graph*

*liker* would be a potential buyer of tickets or memorabilia for that band or other artists with a similar style of music—and so a target for adverts featuring such products.

An individual's participation in social media is driven by different psychological motivation, which may include any of the following reasons:

- People simply *like* to socialize—it is a natural state of affairs for humankind.
- Social media can massage the ego, providing personal validation sought by some people.
- People seek to expand their network of relationships.
- To achieve status within a community.
- Self-expression—on social media the world can read, see, or hear your views.
- To better themselves by seeking knowledge, education, or work.
- To seek out reviews for products from *real people* rather than marketers.
- People can use social media as an avenue for altruistic acts that benefit the community.

Participation in social media does not require a contribution to it, however. Research in 2006 by Jakob Nielsen found that in reality very few users actually contribute, suggesting participation more or less follows the rule that:

- 90 percent are *lurkers*—that is; they read or observe, but don't contribute.
- 9 percent contribute occasionally.
- 1 percent participate a lot and account for most contributions.

Nielsen's findings go on to point out that blogs have an even worse level of participation than his 90-9-1 rule—for them the contribution ratio is more like 95-4.9-0.1. Involvement in Wiki sites is lower again. Wikipedia's most active thousand contributors—0.003 percent of its users—contribute around two-thirds of the site's edits. Nielsen maintains that the figures have changed little since then, with empirical evidence and a lack of contradictory research suggesting he is correct. Although *lurking* on some sites can be explained as being entertained (e.g., watching videos posted by others), information search (e.g., reading reviews), or voyeurism (e.g., watching or reading about the actions of others), much of it is explained by a phenomenon known as social validation, or—more commonly in the digital environment—social *proof*. With foundations in societal behavior (etiquette at a formal occasion, or simply following the herd, for example), social proof is the emotional experience people face when unaware of the socially acceptable behavior in a given circumstance or event. This leads them to seek guidance and/or validation from those they consider to be peers. Although a societal issue within social media, the concept is significant for those seeking to practice marketing in social media in that it explains—among other things—the wary customer seeking the reviews or opinions of others (on social media) before making a buying decision. This commercialization of social proof was led by Robert Cialdini who, in his 1983 book *Influence: The Psychology of Persuasion* lists social proof (people will do things that they see other people are doing) as one of the *six weapons of influence* that can be used in persuasive marketing. Potential customers seeking the views of peers prior before committing to a purchase have given rise to the phenomenon of people trusting *someone like me* rather than marketing messages. Indeed, the notion that people trust other people (more than marketers) has been advanced by Reichelt et al. (2014) who found that trustworthiness emerged as predominant in electronic word-of-mouth (eWOM), with positive impacts on both the utilitarian and the social function of eWOM. Reichelt's research included more bad news for marketers in that it determined that the person seeking the message trusted a peer with limited knowledge of the product's attributes, uses, or applications rather than the company selling the product that might be expected to know far more about the product.

If Nielsen set the ball rolling with his description of some social media users as *lurkers*, others have been quick to pick up that ball and run for the end zone. Many personality types to describe users of social media have been proposed, but one that seems to hit more than it misses was developed as part of a research project by First Direct (2013). Its suggestion for the new breed of social media personas included the following:

- *Ultras* are fanatically obsessed with the likes of Facebook and Twitter, they use smartphone apps to check their social media pages dozens of times a day—even when they should be doing something else, such as work.
- *Deniers* claim social media doesn't control their lives, but the reality is it does.
- *Dippers* access their pages infrequently, often going days—or even weeks—without engaging.
- *Virgins* sign up to social networks but struggle initially to get to grips with the workings of the various platforms, but they may go on to become *ultras*.
- *Lurkers* (thank you, Mr Nielsen) are hiding in the shadows of cyberspace, they rarely participate in social media conversations, perhaps because they worry about having nothing interesting to say.
- *Peacocks* are easily recognized because they love to show everyone how popular they are. They compete with friends for followers or fans, or how many *likes* or re-tweets they get.
- *Ranters* are meek and mild in face-to-face conversation, but are highly opinionated online. Social media allows them to have strong opinions without worrying how others will react in face-to-face confrontations.
- *Ghosts* are worried about giving out personal information to strangers, so they create usernames to stay anonymous or have noticeably sparse profiles and timelines.
- *Changelings* go beyond being anonymous—adopting very different personalities, confident in the knowledge that no one knows their real identity.
- *Quizzers* like to ask questions on social media in order to start conversations and so avoid the risk of being left out.
- *Informers* are the first to spot interesting information, earn kudos and—importantly—more followers and fans by disseminating it.

- *Approval-seekers* worry about how many *likes*, comments, re-tweets, and so on that they get and, because they associate endorsement with popularity, constantly check their feeds and timelines.

Do you recognize yourself? Or are you not willing to recognize yourself? I will admit that the closest of these to my social media personality is that of *dipper*. However, with regard to building the background knowledge required to write a book on the subject, I *lurk* more than might be considered healthy.

Zhu and Chen (2015) take a different approach, presenting the public's use of social media as a matrix (shown in Table 2.1) dividing the various platforms into those that address content- and profile-based against customized and broadcast messages. Note that Zhu and Chen's matrix refers only to social use of social media and not how marketers use it for different kinds of message. We will revisit this matrix in the final chapter.

Research into how people use social media is manifold—with a concentration on its societal use. An extensive study for Childnet International (2008), for example, resulted in multiple reasons for using social media—but none could be described as having any connection with an organization, brand, or product's social media marketing efforts (e.g., there was no mention of seeking product information, or reviews of a service). This reflects a notion that has pervaded digital marketing since

*Table 2.1  The social media matrix (Zhu and Chen 2015)*

|  | Customized message | Broadcast message |
|---|---|---|
| **Profile-based** | Relationship<br><br>Allows users to connect, reconnect, communicate, and build relationships (e.g., Facebook). | Self-media<br><br>Allows users to broadcast their updates and others to follow (e.g., Twitter). |
| **Content-based** | Collaboration<br><br>Allows users to collaboratively find answers, advice, and help (e.g., Reddit). | Creative outlet<br><br>Allows users to share their interest, creativity, and hobbies with each other (e.g., Pinterest). |

social media became *chic*. That is: when users go to search engines (e.g., Google), e-commerce sites (e.g., Wal-Mart), and third-party retail platforms (e.g., eBay) they are in *buyer* mode—making them receptive to marketing messages. But they visit social media sites in *social* mode, making them unreceptive to marketing messages.

I'll end this section with some academic research from the field of psychology—in particular, narcissism. A paper by McCain and Campbell (2016) revealed that grandiose narcissism, the more extroverted, callous form (of narcissism), positively related to time spent on social media, the frequency of updates, number of friends/followers, and the frequency of posting selfies. Now why does that not surprise me?

## 2.2 What Platforms Are Out There?

Here's my list of social media sites circa summer 2017:

About.me, Academia.edu, Advogato, Airtime, Amazon Spark, aNobii, AsianAve, Ask.fm, Athlinks, Audimated, Badoo, Baidu Tieba, Bebo, Biip.no, BlackPlanet, Busuu, BuzzNet, Cabana, CafeMom, Care2, CaringBridge, Cellufun, Classmates, Cloob, ClusterFunk, CouchSurfing, CozCot, Crunchyroll, Cucumbertown, Cyworld, Dailymotion, DailyStrength, delicious, deNA, DeviantArt, Diaspora, Disaboom, Dol-2day, DontStayIn, Draugiem.lv, douban, Doximity, Dreamwidth, DXY. cn, Elftown, Elixio, English, baby!, Entropia Universe, Epernicus, Eons. com, eToro, Experience Project, Exploroo, Facebook, Facebook Workplace, Facebook Spaces, FC2, Fetlife, FilmAffinity, Filmow, FledgeWing, Flixter, Flickr, Focus.com, Fotki, Fotolog, Foursquare, FreshTeam, Friendica, Friendster, Fuelmyblog, Foursquare, Funny or die, Gaia Online, GamerDNA, Gapyear.com, Gather.com, Gays.com, Geni.com, Gentlemint, GetGlue, GirlsAskGuys, GoodReads, Goodwizz, Google+, GREE, Grono.net, Groupon, Habbo, hi5, Hospitality Club, Hotlist, Hub Culture, Ibibo, Identi.ca, Indaba Music, Infield Chatter, Influenster, Instagram, IRC-Galleria, italki.com, Kaixin001, Kiwibox, Last.fm, Late Night Shots, LibraryThing, Lifeknot, Line, Linkagoal, LinkedIn, LinkExpats, Listography, Litsy, LiveJournal, Livemocha, Mastodon, MeetMe, Meettheboss, Meetup, MeWe, MyMFB, Mixi, *MocoSpace, Mottle, MouthShut.com,* MyHeritage, MyLife, My Opera, Myspace, Nasza-klasa.pl, Netlog, Nexopia, Nextdoor, Ning, Odnoklassniki, OUTeverywhere,

PatientsLikeMe, Partyflock, Pingsta, Pinterest, Playlist.com, Plurk, Poolwo, Qzone, Quirky, Raptr, Ravelry, Reddit, Renren, ReverbNation. com, Sina Weibo, Skype, Skyrock, Snapchat, Snapfish, Socl, Sonico, SoundCloud, Spot.IM, Spotify, Stage 32, Streetlife, StudiVZ, Stum-bleUpon, Tagged, Talkbiznow, Taltopia, Taringa, Telegram, TermWiki, TencentQQ, The-dots, The-Sphere, Threadless, Tout, TravBuddy.com, Travellerspoint, tribe.net, Trombi.com, Tsu, Tuenti, Tumblr, Twitter, Uplike, Vampirefreaks, Viadeo, Viber, VK, Vox, Wattpad. wayn, Wechat, WeeWorld, We Heart It, weRead, Whatsapp, Who's In, WriteAPrisoner. com, Xanga, XING, Yammer, Yelp, Yookos, YouTube, YouTube Commu-nity, YY.com, Zoo.gr, Zooppa, and Zynga.

As well as overworking Microsoft Word's spell-check facility on my PC, this list is reasonably comprehensive. However, it does not include all those millions of forums set up for like-minded folk to postulate, argue, seek advice, and generally converse with those who have similar interests. It is also the case that on social media—as in life—nothing lasts forever. As I write this, Twitter has all but pulled the plug on Vine, a darling of *social* only a couple of years before for which Twitter paid a reported $30 million for it in October 2013 and one of the original social media sites, Delicious (whose domain name—del.icio.us—was perhaps the best ever example of the use of a suffix and second level name), seems to be destined for an early grave. Others that have passed on to that social media cloud in the sky include:

- Friendster, launched 2002. Perhaps the first social networking site, even if we didn't recognize it as such at the time, it lived on as a gaming network before closing down completely (although a notice on Friendster.com says it is "taking a break"). I wonder what might it have become of it had the owners not turned down an offer from fellow new start-up Google?
- Myspace, launched 2003. The $580m News Corporation paid for it in 2005 seemed to be a bargain as within 12 months it became the most popular social network. However, Facebook came of age and proved too appealing to Myspacers and by 2008 it was in decline. It was sold in the summer of 2011 for $35m. It does, however, live on—but is a shadow of its former self.
- Friends Reunited, launched 2000. A social networking site in the UK before we knew that there was such a thing as a

social networking site. This really was the introduction to the Internet for a lot of people in the UK and was commonly used in traditional media as an example of what the new online media was bringing to the world. It was purchased by TV company ITV for £175m in 2005—and sold four years later for £25m. Ouch.

- Bebo, launched 2005. The UK's most popular social network in 2007, Bebo was acquired by AOL for $850m in 2008—only to sell it for less than $10m in 2010. Double ouch.

Note to self: if you write another book on the subject in 2027 check the list at the start of this section to see how many still exist.

We should also not forget that many new platforms are yet to make a profit. Perhaps that is why—at the time of writing—Twitter is still scratching around trying to find a buyer? Or perhaps not. When Snapchat went public in February 2017 its impressive stocks went up 44 percent on their first day of trading and valuing the company at $28bn. Not bad for a company that has a record of losing money every year of its existence.

## 2.3 Who Uses Which Platforms?

Previous experience has taught me that if I include here a whole host of statistics drawn from numerous sources on such issues as: how many people use which social media platforms, how often they used them and how long they stayed on them per visit they will have passed their sell-by date before the book reached the shelves (real or virtual). Add in the fact that much of the research is conducted and published by organizations with a vested interest and you have a valid reason for not including any statistics at all. To have none, however, would be remiss so I've included a select few, starting with the excellent Pew Research Center Social Media Update (Greenwood et al. 2016) which comes out at the end of each year—so I should get 12 months out of this data. Here are some of the more notable statistics:

- 79 percent of Internet users (68 percent of all U.S. adults) use Facebook.

- 32 percent of Internet users (28 percent of all U.S. adults) use Instagram.
- 24 percent of Internet users (21 percent of all U.S. adults) use Twitter.
- 29 percent of Internet users (25 percent of all U.S. adults) use LinkedIn.
- 31 percent of Internet users (26 percent of all U.S. adults) use Pinterest.

As might be expected, for all of the five platforms, the usage by 18- to 29-year-olds exceeds the average, with usage dropping as the age groups move up to 30 to 49, and through to 50 to 64 to 65+. Table 2.2 shows the percentage of users for each social media platform who use other platforms.

Facebook not only tops the users' charts, but also that for the frequency of use, as is shown in Figure 2.2.

However, before digital marketers start moving their entire budgets to social media in general and Facebook in particular, in its 32nd semiannual *Taking Stock With Teens* research survey that questions 10,000 teens across 46 U.S. states, PiperJaffray (2016) found that teenagers (average age 16) have fallen out of love with Facebook. That research found that when it

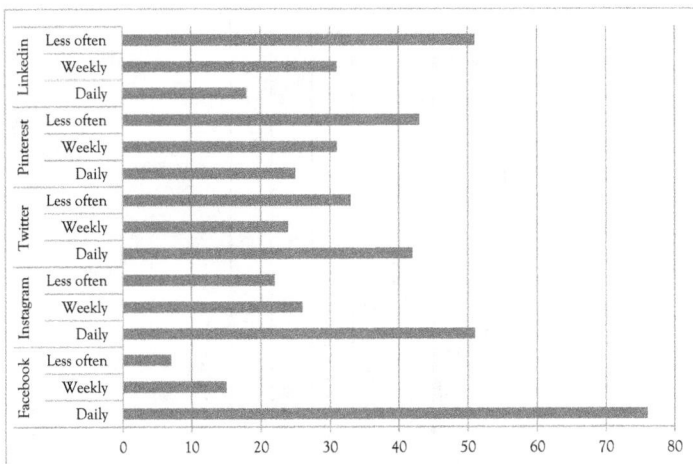

*Figure 2.2  The frequency of use on social media platforms*
Source: Pew Research Center (2016).

**Table 2.2** *Using multiple platforms*

| Using multiple platforms | Use Twitter | Use Instagram | Use Pinterest | Use LinkedIn | Use Facebook |
|---|---|---|---|---|---|
| % of Twitter users who … | | 65 | 48 | 54 | 93 |
| % of Instagram users who … | 49 | | 54 | 48 | 95 |
| % of Pinterest users who … | 38 | 57 | | 41 | 92 |
| % of LinkedIn users who … | 45 | 53 | 43 | | 89 |
| % of Facebook users who … | 29 | 39 | 36 | 33 | |

*Source:* Pew Research Center (2016).

comes to their favorite social media platforms the rankings are: Snap-chat top with 35 percent, Instagram second with 24 percent, and trailing home in joint last place come Twitter and Facebook with 13 percent. If those preferences hold true as these youngsters grow older, Pew's charts are going to look mightily different in coming years. Marketers take note.

More research from Pew Research Center—this time their Global Attitudes Survey released in April 2017—has some rather surprising results (see Figure 2.3). The surprise is just how limited the use of both the Internet and social media is in some countries. Research—and our focus—tends to be on the United States and Northern Europe, but Japan, for example, has 28 percent of its population not using the Internet and in Germany only 37 percent use social media.

Some more numbers that social media marketers need to analyze come from respected commentators, eMarketer (eMarketer.com) who suggest that Facebook reaches around 9 in 10 social network users. That's a great headline statistic, but further down the page comes a qualifica-tion; "on at least a monthly basis." This actually fits with Facebook's own interpretation of *users*. June 2017 saw the social networking Goliath reach the milestone of two billion users. That is, two billion *monthly* users. Of course, there are Facebook *addicts* out there who will visit several times a day, but I wonder how many of those *9 in 10* are in that once-a-month

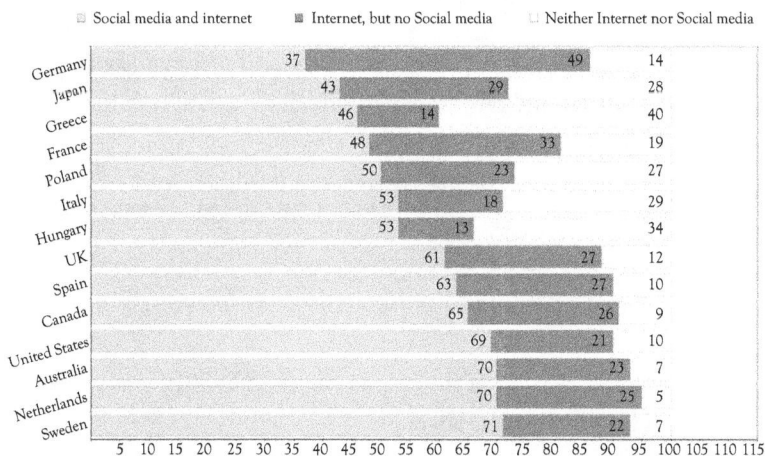

Key:  ▢ Social media and internet    ■ Internet, but no Social media    ▢ Neither Internet nor Social media

| Country | Social media and internet | Internet, but no Social media | Neither Internet nor Social media |
|---|---|---|---|
| Germany | 37 | 49 | 14 |
| Japan | 43 | 29 | 28 |
| Greece | 46 | 14 | 40 |
| France | 48 | 33 | 19 |
| Poland | 50 | 23 | 27 |
| Italy | 53 | 18 | 29 |
| Hungary | 53 | 13 | 34 |
| UK | 61 | 27 | 12 |
| Spain | 63 | 27 | 10 |
| Canada | 65 | 26 | 9 |
| United States | 69 | 21 | 10 |
| Australia | 70 | 23 | 7 |
| Netherlands | 70 | 25 | 5 |
| Sweden | 71 | 22 | 7 |

*Figure 2.3 The use of the Internet and social media in various countries*

Source: Pew Research Center (2016).

group because—let's be realistic—"once a month" could be interpreted as "don't really use Facebook."

Research by Childnet International (2008) identified that many social media users sign up to social media platforms for the sole purpose of seeing content posted by others. The example given was that of photo-sharing site Flickr, where *empty* accounts are used to view their friends' or family's permission-protected pictures. Furthermore, could it be that a significant number of users have signed up to image-related platforms (e.g., Flickr, Instagram, and Snapchat) for one-off events—photos of weddings or vacations, for example? If such users do not cancel their membership (why would they?) they remain as part of the user numbers for those platforms. Essentially, not only more proof of the 90-9-1 rule, but a reminder that platform user statistics should be treated with caution—if not skepticism—with regard to those users being genuine targets for social media marketing.

Similarly, there are millions of blogs floating around in cyberspace that have only ever been read by their authors—who last added a post many years ago. Tracking them down would be an impossible task, but that is not the case for Twitter "tweets" which are easier to track from sender to those who read them—or more accurately, don't read them. Research from Twitter analysts Twopcharts[1] (2014) supports Nielsen's rule, the key elements of which included that:

- Less than half of the Twitter accounts (46.8 percent) have a profile image and only 23.9 percent have a description for their account profile.
- 44 percent of the existing Twitter accounts have never sent a tweet.
- 30 percent of accounts have sent between 1 and 10 tweets.
- 13 percent of accounts have sent 100 or more tweets in their history.
- Around 11 percent of the accounts created in 2012 are tweeting a little over a year later.

---

[1] Twopcharts.com

It is perhaps noteworthy that Twitter didn't comment on Twopcharts' report—read into that what you will. I'm far from being proficient at math, but the 90-9-1 rule doesn't look to be too far out in these statistics.

Simply by comparing data from multiple sources, Tim Peterson (Third Door Media's social media reporter) has also shed some light on the *who might read what is posted* conundrum, this time regarding Instagram. In an article on Marketingland.com,[2] he deduced that only around two-thirds of Instagram's daily audience swipe past the *Stories* (a feature that lets users post photos and videos that vanish after 24 hours) that sit conspicuously on top of the platform's main feeds. The flip side to this is that the one-third that do view the *Stories* represent around 100 million, so maybe they're not too upset. A postscript to these numbers is that Instagram is owned by Facebook, who—as I write—is facing severe criticism from advertisers *and* the attention of the Media Ratings Council (MRC) amid speculation that the social media giant's own reporting cannot be trusted following a series of mistakes in the validation of its own metrics.

I do have a couple of personal experiences of the Twitter *sent* versus *read* issue. The first dates back to the back end of 2009 when I set up my first Twitter account. It immediately gathered followers—far beyond my expectations—but as I say in my online musing of the story[3]:

Sadly, self-congratulation soon turned to disappointment as new followers dropped me just as quickly.

A quick check revealed a few *genuine* followers have stayed with me over the six months I have twittered (around 20—and six are ex-students). Now, I do appreciate that some (all?) dropped out because they saw no value in my tweets, but (a) they knew what they were signing up for, and (b) a week and two tweets is hardly time to form a judgment before jumping ship.

So why did these folk elect to *follow* me? My conclusion is that they are all *follower whores* who are simply trying to achieve high *follower* numbers. Further analysis of my Twitter account shows that the vast majority of my *joiners* both follow, and are followed by, significant numbers. They

---

[2] http://marketingland.com/instagram-stories-get-viewed-%E2%85%93-300-million-large-daily-audience-ignored-%E2%85%94-194197

[3] See www.alancharlesworth.eu/alans-musings/what-tweeting-use-is-twitter.html

also have little or no interest in Internet marketing. The key to the issue is in the e-mail sent telling you of a new follower. It says: "You may follow [their name] as well by clicking on the *follow* button on their profile." Yes, I'm supposed to reward new followers by following them. I don't—so I'm quickly dropped.

And, of course, this is the Internet—where there is software for every occasion. In reality, these folk don't actually visit my Twitter page to sign up—they send Twitter *followbots* to automatically follow users (in my case, it seems randomly, though they can be targeted to demographic data or use of keywords) in the hope that users will *follow* them in return.

Need some numbers? Of my 65 short-term twitterers, the average number of *twits* they were *following* was 5,852 and were *followed by* 6,043. Some bloke in New England topped the list with 43,980 and 44,443 respectively. If each *followed* member sent him only one tweet a week that is 261 every hour. Are you telling me that this guy has time to read all the tweets that land in his account?

Within a couple of months I stopped using that Twitter page but did not close the account—posting on it the message: "I'm giving up on this Twitter malarkey," and I've added nothing since then. That did not, however, stop nearly 300 users choosing to follow a *dead* twitterer—enough to prove my point about *follow-bots* and *Twitter whores*?

The second example is more recent, and comes from a source I use to keep me up-to-date with what is actually happening out there in the digital marketing world, clickz.com. One article from July 2016 gave a list of "100+ marketing leaders you should follow on Twitter.[4]" Now, I have no issue with the list, or even the concept of offering a list of people to follow—not everyone has been around as long as me, we all need help when getting started. Neither do I have any problem with the fact that I'm not on the list (another smiley face). My point is this: I have a professional interest in all of the subjects listed and so might decide to follow them all. If each of these *leaders* tweeted just once a week, that equates to around 14 tweets a day—with each tweet probably linked to an article to look at. I'll let you do the math for the numbers if they tweeted more

---

[4] www.clickz.com/102-marketing-leaders-you-should-follow-on-twitter/102636/

often, say once a day. So, (a) when am I supposed to find the time to read all of these things, and (b) what about any other sources I already follow? Plus I'm in a job where part of that job is to keep myself updated on the subject—what if you are busy digitally marketing all day?' Nuff said?

And these issues aren't limited to Twitter. Because—frankly—life is too short, I have not kept track of the numbers, but hardly a day goes by that I do not receive a "so-and-so wants to join your network" e-mail from LinkedIn. They may not be robots, but if I do not know *so-and-so* in real life I simply reject their request. Again, I am assuming that a reciprocal request is expected so that the *requester* can build his or her own LinkedIn profile.

If you want to take a look at who follows whom on Facebook and Twitter, spend a few minutes on Fanpage.com.

Beyond the Pew Research Center findings is a plethora of un-referenced commentators from recent years that I think is worth your consideration. I should add that my own, very much ad-hoc and un-scientific research supports these observations.[5]

- Plenty of folk use social networking sites, but only around a third of those rate social media as being *important* to them.
- Adults who are currently a member of more than one social networking site are overloaded and/or overwhelmed with multiple social accounts and half have either taken or are considered taking a vacation from one or more social networks.
- While women are highly active and influential on social media, they are also more likely to decrease or completely stop usage of at least one social network.
- People abandoning social media cite four main reasons for quitting: privacy concerns lead the way at around 50 percent, general dissatisfaction and negative aspects of online friends at around 15 percent each are followed by 6 percent fearing that they may become addicted.

---

[5] It's a personal view; but I think that *informal* discussions on a subject with people —often as part of wider-ranging conversations—can be far more revealing by way of research than presenting them with a series of questions in a *formal* questionnaire.

- People are more likely to *share* images than textual content.

Do you recognize yourself in any of these?

## 2.4 Why People Follow Social Media Sites of Organizations, Brands, or Products

Research into this subject abound; I have chosen to include a representative sample here. The first is from SUMO Heavy Industries (2016), which revealed some interesting information on why users are on social media (see Table 2.3).

Note how small a role *finding specific information on products and services* has in the use of social media. Furthermore, the same research found that, when asked about what influences consumers about a brand and its products, 56 percent said "family members" and "friends" posts. Add to that statistics that 62 percent have shared information about products and offers on social media, and it becomes a reasonable conclusion that when users are looking for product information they are looking on the pages of friends and family as much—if not more—than brands' pages. In addition to this rather gloomy news for social media marketers, the same research also found that advertisements and sponsored

Table 2.3 *Why users are on social media*

| Reasons | Younger users <29 yrs | Older users 30 yrs+ |
|---|---|---|
| Friends and family | 87% | 77% |
| Pass time | 72% | 42% |
| Stay informed on news | 65% | 41% |
| Entertainment | 57% | 28% |
| Share personal information and content | 52% | 33% |
| Learn about people | 38% | 21% |
| Find specific information on products and services | 28% | 22% |
| Meet new people | 24% | 6% |

*Source:* SUMO Heavy Industries (2016).

*Table 2.4 Why consumers follow brands on social media*

|  | Facebook | Twitter | Pinterest | YouTube | Instagram |
|---|---|---|---|---|---|
| Keep up with activities | 52% | 57% | 35% | 41% | 41% |
| Learn about product/service | 56% | 47% | 56% | 61% | 39% |
| Sweepstakes/ promotions | 48% | 36% | 28% | 20% | 23% |
| Provide helpful feedback | 32% | 27% | 22% | 23% | 22% |
| Join community of brand fans | 27% | 26% | 25% | 19% | 19% |
| To complain about product/ service | 18% | 19% | 12% | 9% | 15% |

*Source:* Technorati Media (2013).

posts influence less than 16 percent of social media users. Based on these numbers some might question the use of the medium at all as an effective marketing tool. Or might they be questioning just how the Emperor looks in his new clothes?

Technorati Media[6] (2013) concentrated on five leading social media platforms; Facebook, Twitter, YouTube, Pinterest, and Instagram. The key findings are shown in Table 2.4.

Marketers should be aware of these motives so that expectations are met. Many are self-evident and—as we will discover in later chapters— pertinent to whatever the organization does, what industry it is in, what the brand represents, or what the product or service is. Nevertheless, there are issues for marketers, not least that *joining a community of brand fans* sits so low down the list. Shouldn't this be what social media is all about? One thing that—in theory—social media is *not* about is promotions for the brand. That is: advertising. To use a social media presence merely to

---

[6] At the time Technorati's focus was on the use of social media in marketing. Since then it has moved to being "advertising technology specialists," which perhaps explains why 2013 was the last of a series of excellent annual reports on social media.

host promotions does not equate to the ethos of social media marketing
… but that, it would seem, is the reason many people follow brands.

Social media software suppliers, Sprout Social, provide some more
up-to-date statistics in their Sprout Social Index (2016). Their research
included: the actions that make people follow a brand on social media
(see Figure 2.4), annoying actions brands take on social media (see
Figure 2.5), and actions that make people un-follow a brand on social

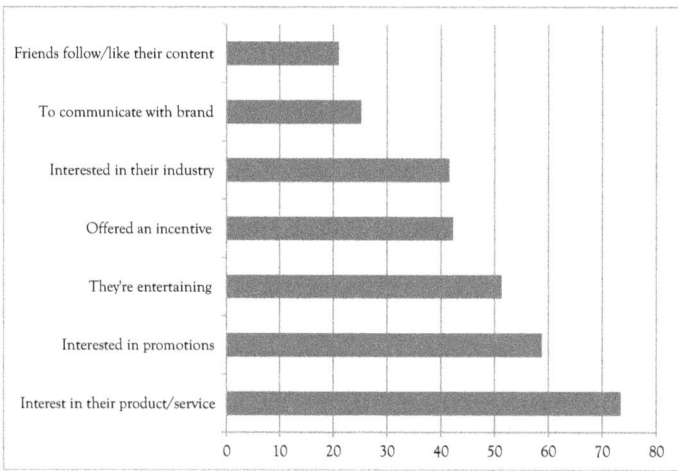

*Figure 2.4  Actions that make people follow a brand on social media*

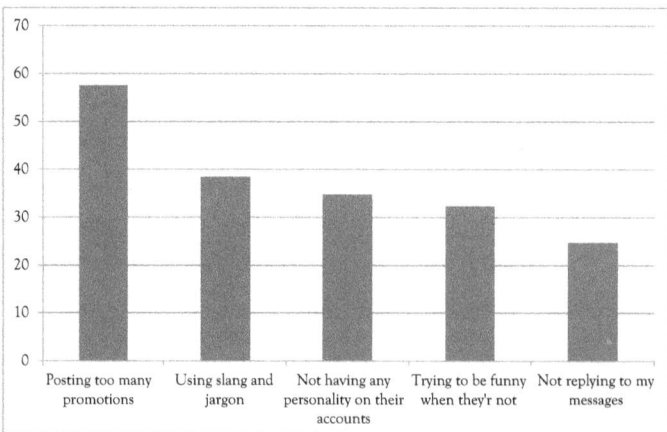

*Figure 2.5  Annoying actions brands take on social media*

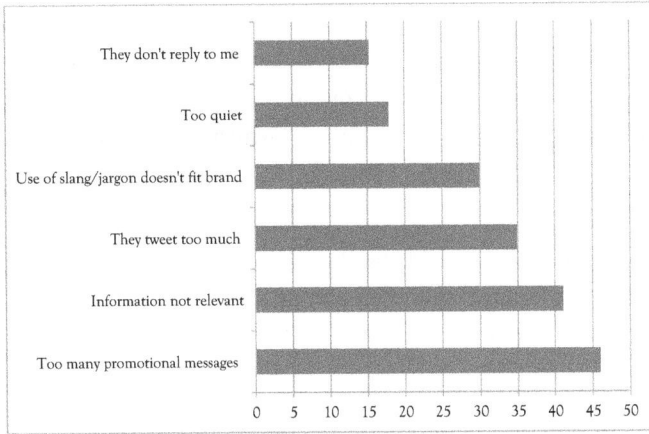

*Figure 2.6  Actions that make people un-follow a brand on social media*

media (see Figure 2.6). Note the strong correlation between what annoys people and what incites them to un-follow a brand.

Although it offers a more comprehensive range of reasons for respondents to choose from in expressing why they might follow a brand on social media, these results are strikingly similar to those of Technorati Media in that there seems to be a preponderance of folk joining to enhance their bank balance than truly social purposes. That around half seek some kind of entertainment is interesting—as is the power of peers. And what about the 42 percent who joined up for an incentive? I'm going to call that *buying friends* and leave it to you to decide just how loyal *they* are going to be to a brand.

As with the Technorati findings, there is a certain irony that so many people are annoyed by the frequency of promotions and choose to un-follow a brand because of it and yet 58.8 percent joined for promotions in the first place. That so many followers decide that the jargon/slang doesn't fit the brand, the content has no personality or it is trying to be funny and failing suggests the brand has got its *voice* wrong, something covered in more detail in Chapter 5 (Section 5.2). Indeed, all of the reasons listed suggest that the brand simply does not *get* social media—which is a subject that presides over the book's contents from the next chapter through to the last.

Sprout Social's research also found that 70 percent of people have *un-followed* a brand because they were embarrassed that their friends might see they were following it. Compelling evidence perhaps that: (a) social media is fickle, it follows trends—and drops them just as quickly, and (b) peer pressure plays a major role in social media, which suggests a certain lack of self-confidence in users—which is relevant to marketers. And rather sad for humanity.

Furthermore, if we combine the data from SUMO Heavy Industries with that from Technorati Media and Sprout Social we have a reasonable conclusion that if only around 25 percent of users go on social media to find out about a product or service (and they may well go to friends' or family's pages for that information) that doesn't leave a significant proportion of all users who are actually engaging in the activities described in the findings of Technorati Media and Sprout Social. The roundup of research data on the subject gets no better for marketers if that of Kumar et al. (2016) is accurate. They calculated that the percentage of a customer base that participates in a firm's social media sites ranges from 1.00 percent to 7.35 percent, with an average of 3.7 percent. This group's research combined their primary data with other secondary data to arrive at these figures, so there is no reason to cast doubt on them. But even if they were 100 percent out and the real figure is around 7 percent, that's not really very many of the brands customers that are engaging with the organization on social media. A more pessimistic person might actually stop reading this book at this point as they consider that these numbers suggest any social media marketing would not give a reasonable return on any investment. For those *glass-half-full* people, stay with us, there is better news. Later in the book I raise the argument that some organizations, brands, or products are culturally better suited for social media marketing. One such brand is Starbucks, and its 36,549,320[7] Facebook followers must represent more than 3.7 percent of its customer base.

It is my contention that the majority who choose to follow an organization, brand, or product do so because they are already a satisfied customer. In terms of being a customer in its most literal definition—by which I mean people purchase a product—Starbucks would be an excellent example. Why would anyone *like* the ubiquitous coffee provider

---

[7] *Source*: Fanpagelist.com, January 8, 2017.

if they hadn't sampled the product? Research from Brodie et al. (2013) finds in favor of my contention, arguing that customers who engage with brand communities online feel more connected to their brands, trust their preferred brands more, are more committed to their chosen brands, have higher brand satisfaction, and are more brand loyal. More recently, Sprout Social (2017) found that 62 percent of people said they are likely or somewhat likely to purchase a product from a brand they follow on social media. Bagozzi and Dholakia (2006) also found that consumers who become fans of these brand fan pages tend to be loyal and committed to the company, and are more open to receiving information about the brand. My contention is that this is precisely why they are *fans*.

Further evidence of this comes from what I feel is the best *academic* journal because it isn't too academic—the *Harvard Business Review*. John et al. (2017) challenged the concept that people who liked a Facebook page routinely spent more with that brand by questioning cause and consequence, investigating the possibility that "those who already have positive feelings toward a brand are more likely to follow it in the first place, and that's why they spend more than *non-followers*." Although they identified that supporting endorsements with branded content can have significant results, "the mere act of endorsing a brand does not affect a customer's behavior or lead to increased purchasing, nor does it spur purchasing by friends."

In effect, we are looking at whether or not people are predisposed to have a relationship with an organization, brand, or product. This is something I have questioned with regard to the concept of relationship marketing—of which social media marketing is at least a relative, but more likely an element. Here's the thing: people do not necessarily want a relationship with an organization, brand, or product—why would they? Take a look at the aforementioned Fanpagelist site to see how poorly brands fare in the *follow* and *like* leagues—and don't forget the percentage of folk who *like* firms purely for the discount coupons. Research by Dixon and Ponomareff supports this premise—the title of their 2010 *Harvard Business Review* article making their case. In "Why Your Customers Don't Want to Talk to You" the authors make the point that customers these days demonstrate a huge appetite for self-service—the result of their preference not to interact with the sellers. So if a customer would rather use an ATM than a bank teller, why would that same customer want a *relationship* with that bank? Not for the only time in this book I put forward the assertion that if it is the *right* product in the *right* place at the *right* time, then most—all?—customers will not only buy a product but make repeat purchases. Interestingly, the research by SUMO Heavy Industries in 2016 found that if customers *loved* their purchase, 83 percent would share it on Facebook. By definition, a relationship is two-sided with both parties having to perceive an advantage to the union. Businesses want a relationship with me to sell me more goods. Well, provide me with the *right* product in the *right* place at the *right* price and I will continue to buy your goods. If I get the wrong choice of product; *or* it isn't where I want to buy it; *or* its price doesn't meet my valuation then no amount of *relationship* will encourage me to remain a customer. Always happy to put my own head above the digital parapet, here's an example of my own experience with regard to relationships with brands.

This illustration is prompted by a report[8] that Toyota is way ahead of its rivals when it comes to Twitter engagement, in particular its *Go Fun Yourself* campaign that was delivered in off- and online media. Now, although perhaps a little old, I am most definitely in the target segment for Toyota's only *sports* coupe (the GT86/Scion FR-S) and it is sold as a *fun* car rather than a *sensible*, boring, go-from-A-to-B mode of transport. I have also owned Toyota cars for 20 of the last 27 years. And I have owned one particular type of Toyota sports car for 15 years and around a quarter of a million driven miles. I still have one of these now, it is 30 years old. That suggests I am a stronger *supporter* of Toyota than your average car owner. I also accept that—as the article accurately portrays—Toyota's social media team is doing a fine job. But for the life of me I cannot think of a single reason why I would want a social media *relationship* with Toyota, that is; read dozens of Tweets that have no interest to me whatsoever. If I buy another Toyota, social media will play no role in my purchase decision or behavior. OK, I might read some owner reviews, but I will take more notice of *professional* reviews. Ultimately, if I like the look of the car (essential), and its interior meets my user expectations

---

[8] https://econsultancy.com/blog/65714-how-toyota-beats-24-other-car-brands-in-twitter-engagement

(essential—I have a back problem, the seats are a deal-breaker for me) and if I like the way it drives—that is; if the car is *right* for me, and if I can buy it and get it serviced locally and if the price meets what I value the car to be worth to me, then I might buy one. Of course that could be just me, and I do appreciate a less *petrolhead* buyer than me might be more susceptible to a social media marketing relationship, but I do wonder just how many cars Twitter engagement *actually* sells. Note that return on social media marketing investment is covered in Chapter 4.

Beyond my assertion of Starbucks being an example of customers supporting the brand, it would be remiss to ignore the softer characterization of being a *customer* of an organization, brand, or product. The data would suggest that many people do follow brands and that some do so prior to making a purchase. For example, the aforementioned Sprout Social (2017) research found that 58.9 percent of Millennials, 50.4 percent of Generation X-ers, and 55 percent of Baby Boomers have all followed a brand on social media *before* purchasing a product. The Sprout report does not give details of its methodology, and so I resorted to my own research to shed some light on this—after all, it does contradict my earlier assertion that there is no reason for anyone *liking* an organization, brand, or product if they hadn't sampled the product?

As with most of my primary research, this was conducted in ad hoc rather than scientific fashion, but I did identify over 100 students who had *liked* or *followed* an organization, brand, or product on social media— though this was not easy; a significant number of folk have never done so. As it turned out, the answer to the conundrum came to me as I asked the respondents why they *liked* or *followed* an organization, brand, or product. Before answering they asked me to define *organization*, *brand*, or *product*, specifically; "are people, performers, movies and games brands?" This would be the issue I would raise with Sprout's research—not, I hasten to add, to criticize it, just to clarify the results for my own purposes. I have to admit that when I envisage a product it is a physical product (i.e., that I use, eat, or drink) and a brand is the name on some of those products—but I'm being too simplistic. When I questioned the students (in a series of focus groups) I found that they all followed music artists, movie stars, celebrities, and comedians, the latter being very popular as postings were normally funny. In other words, following wasn't *engagement* with the brand (person), it was a source of entertainment. Also popular at the time of the interviews was the movie, and stars of, *La La Land* (ironically the sessions sandwiched the movie's gain and loss of the best picture award at the Oscars). Also very popular were multiplayer video games, some of which require a certain social media interaction to be fully engaged. Also popular were entertainment channels such as Netflix and Spotify as well as niche radio stations. Finally there was the one that saw me slapping my forehead in a well duh! moment: news channels. I tend to access the BBC on the radio, TV, or web. I had totally forgotten (because I don't use them) that the BBC has a Facebook page for breaking news and Twitter accounts that will notify you of personalized news, about your sports teams, for example. For the majority of readers of this book, replace BBC with a U.S. national or local news provider of your choice. It is my opinion that examples such as these artificially boost engagement figures—they are clear exponent of Jacob Nielsen's 90-9-1 rule and—as I will address later in the book—they are not *true* social media marketing. They might also give some rationalization to the research that so many people *follow* before purchase—*liking* the *La La Land* Facebook page before visiting a cinema to watch the movie, for example.

# CHAPTER 3

# What Is Social Media Marketing?

*Take everything you like seriously, except yourselves*

In the rather contradictory manner of other aspects of this book, I'm going to start a chapter titled *what is social media marketing* with a section detailing what social media marketing is *not* when it is not *social media marketing*. Furthermore, the second section of the chapter considers when social media marketing is social media marketing. Confused? Hopefully not by the time you have finished the chapter.

## 3.1 What Is Social Media Marketing Not?

I would suggest that the following points are at the core of the Emperor's New *Digital* Clothes and so the *not* issue is important. Here's what it is *not*.

1. Social media marketing is *not* a magic bullet for all the woes of every organization, brand and, product. Or put another way—if is not too cheap a reference to the book's title—it is not the panacea to all the business and marketing problems, ailments, and issues for every organization, brand, and product known to mankind.

2. Social media marketing is *not* free. This issue pervades all subsequent chapters of this book. To paraphrase Mark Twain; *reports that social media marketing is free are greatly exaggerated*. Just to make myself clear—social media marketing is not, nor ever was, *free*. This deeply flawed proposition originated, presumably, from the fact that setting up a Facebook page or a blog (on the likes of Blogger.com) incurs no charge. And if the social media content you develop and publish is personal (i.e., not commercial), then it costs you only your free time.

However, if that Facebook page or blog *is* commercial, that is; it is part of the marketing for an organization, brand, person, entity, or product—then the development time is chargeable. If nothing else, there is the opportunity cost of doing something else in the time spent developing the social media content.

3. Social media marketing is *not* advertising on social media platforms. Advertising on social media platforms is *advertising*. Conversely, if you have a Facebook page, that is not advertising. It is social media marketing. The objectives, required skills, management—indeed, everything else covered in subsequent chapters of this book—for effective social media marketing are very different to those required for effective online advertising. Consider also that the same ad can appear elsewhere online, search engine results pages (SERPs) for example. I find it extremely frustrating that folk talking or writing about social media marketing include advertising on platforms such as Facebook or Twitter as part of the discipline. We don't call advertising on TV, TV marketing, we call it TV advertising. We don't call advertising on radio, radio marketing, we call it radio advertising. We don't call advertising in out-of-home formats, out-of-home marketing, we call it out-of-home advertising (OOHA). So why do we call advertising on social media platforms social media *marketing*? I think there are two key reasons, though the second may be a result of the first. As I cover in more detail in Chapter 5 (Section 5.1), a great many of the people working in all aspects of digital marketing are not *marketers*. That is, they have no marketing experience or education. Often from technical backgrounds, they have mastered an element of digital marketing (search engine optimization or programmatic advertising, for example) but they do not know how it fits in with other aspects of digital marketing or understand how that aspect of digital marketing fits in with strategic marketing objectives. Hence, we have people working in social media marketing who do not appreciate that there is a difference between advertising and marketing. The second reason is that marketers—and people who write books about marketing— like to have things in nice clean categories because they make for

convenient departments or chapters. Ergo, anything with any connection to social media is social media marketing. I prefer to categorize by disciplines so, in my digital marketing books, *online advertising* covers advertising on all of the different platforms that accommodate it, including websites, search engine results pages, *and* social media pages. Essentially they are all an aspect of *programmatic network advertising*—and that is not a subject that has any place in a book on social media marketing. A caveat to this is that on Facebook (and coming soon on all other platforms?) marketers can pay to *boost* a post. Some call this advertising; I would call it a promotion (in marketing terms, advertising is part of the promotional mix) if only so it does not get mixed up with *advertising* on Facebook. If you can have a caveat to a caveat, here is one. Some folk call the practice of boosting posts *paid social*; and some call advertising on social media *paid social*. And some call *any* social media practice that involves payment of a fee *paid social*. We do seem to weave an unnecessarily tangled web at times. Another issue with regard to advertising on social media platforms is the common failing for marketers, researchers, writers, and commentators to differentiate between social media marketing and advertising on social media. I frequently come across managers who say they conduct social media marketing, only to discover they advertise on social media. We also need to consider the methodology of some research and how it defines *social media marketing*. A statistic that reads (something like) "more videos are shown on social media than other online platforms" for example, takes on a different context if video ads are included or excluded.

A final point on the subject that has relevance to the Emperor's New *Digital* Clothes syndrome is how it too—like social media marketing itself—tends to fall victim to overhyping. Social media advocates (can I interest you in a new set of clothes sir?) would have us believe that *social* is the home of both video in general and the video ad. In the UK at least this is not the case—I suspect these statistics are not so different to what they might be for the United States.

According to research from Thinkbox,[1] the marketing body for commercial TV in the UK, TV accounted for 74.8 percent of all videos viewed and a whopping 93.8 percent of video ads viewed in the UK in 2016 (note that these could be watched either live, playback, or on a broadcaster's video on demand service) so despite all the talk of how *digital* is taking over the marketing world, perhaps the old style of clothes that consumers can actually see are still the best option for that ever-diminishing marketing budget?

## 3.2 When Is Social Media Marketing *Not* Social Media Marketing?

It is, perhaps, a reflection of the popularity—or whisper it quietly—the spread of the Emperor's New *Digital* Clothes, that social media marketing is given credit for any and all marketing campaigns that have any connection or association with social media. For example, the streaming of live events to be watched on mobile devices is generally attributed as being to social media marketing. The reason for this is that the platforms used for such events are often YouTube or Facebook Live, both of which are stalwarts of social media. I am—if somewhat reluctantly—willing to accept this as social media marketing, and so it is included at the end of this chapter. My caveat, however, is that the broadcast must be hosted on a third-party social media platform. For example; when, in November 2016, denim apparel manufacturer Wrangler teamed up with George Strait in showing a live stream of the country music icon's return to the stage for the first time in 34 years, it is not surprising that it was promoted as being social media marketing. After all, it was live streaming of an event. It was produced to be watched on mobile devices. Sounds like social media marketing doesn't it? But the broadcast was hosted on Wrangler's own media hub (a website, wranglernetwork.com), not on a third-party platform. Therefore, although it may be considered to be

---

[1] Thinkbox's (Thinkbox.tv) video analysis combined 2016 data from The Broadcasters' Audience Research Board (BARB), comScore, the IPA's Touchpoints 2016 study, Ofcom's 2016 Digital Day study, and Rentrak box office data to give a like for like comparison of estimated video consumption in the UK.

*digital* marketing, is it social media marketing? In traditional marketing terms: is it *simply* sponsorship? However, closer inspection of the details suggests that the event was part of an agreement between Wrangler and Universal Music Group Nashville whereby the former has exclusive rights to broadcast content from the latter. Now that sounds more like a strategic business deal than social media marketing.

Further examples of *faux* social media marketing from the latter months of 2016 include:

- IHOP restaurants' photo contest to win a year's worth of breakfast as part of its *Eat Up Every Moment* campaign. Photo contests have been a staple of marketing since photography was invented. That Twitter, Facebook, or Instagram were used to enter a picture into the competition makes social media the mode of entry to a competition, not the type of marketing.
- To launch new mint and strawberry cheesecake flavors, Oreo used a social influencer—with over four million views on Facebook—to promote the launch. This was old-school promotion using a celebrity endorsement, not a new concept in marketing made possible only by the invention of online social media.
- Jack Daniel's Tennessee Whiskey USA Barrel Hunt contest was an old-fashioned scavenger hunt—but one where the clues were posted on its Facebook page rather than any other form of publication.
- In December 2016, ABC announced that fans of "The Bachelor" would have another way to keep in touch with the happenings thanks to the introduction of a new Snapchat companion show called "Watch Party." My take on this is that "Watch Party" is a TV program broadcast on a social media platform. It is not social media marketing—though I do appreciate that the Snapchat show might encourage other social media engagement.
- In late December (the 29th, it couldn't have been much later) 2016, the National Football League announced that it would be streaming games on China's premier social media network Sina Weibo. That is a live broadcast, not social media marketing.

As with many aspects of the subject, the association to social media of these strategies and campaigns is promoted by social media marketing departments and agencies as being part of their remit. Given that budgets depend on such things it is hard to blame them, but that is rather harsh on all the other marketing folk who would have been involved in—for example—the development and marketing (packaging, TV advertising, in-store promotion) for the new Oreo flavors mentioned previously.

The final *this is not* social media marketing goes under the rather sinister name of *dark social*. The term confuses some as it is associated with the *dark web*—something that really does have sinister overtones as it often linked to illegal or dubious activities. Dark social, on the other hand, is the description given to *social* messages sent directly to the recipient (normally by either e-mail, the personal massage facility on a social media platform, or a messaging app) that are not placed in a public space such as Facebook. That only the addressee sees the message has resulted in these e-mails and personal or app messages being dubbed *dark social*—as in: not visible to everyone. The association with *social* comes from the *dark* messages being in response to a communication on social media. For example a question posed in a public forum is answered by e-mail or personal message. There are two aspects to this for the organization to consider, depending on who is the recipient of the *dark* social message.

1. The *dark* message is sent by consumers to other consumers via e-mail or personal message; for example, "the product on this Facebook page is great/rubbish, buy it/don't buy it." In this scenario the social media marketers have lost track of the conversation. The conversation is out in the wind. In marketing terms it is *word-of-mouth*, a subject mentioned in the next section of this chapter.

2. The *dark* message is sent via e-mail or personal message by the consumers to the marketer. For example, "could you tell me if the product on this Facebook page is available in my city?" or "I have a problem with your product, can you help?" However, it is important to note that such a message should not be considered to be social media marketing as the contact is between an individual and the organization in a private conversation, not one conducted in the public arena of a social media platform. In just the same way as it

would in the *real world*, when communication switches from public to private, not only does the whole tone and nature of that conversation change, but different skills to those practiced on social media are required to address the consumer's personal query. In these two examples, the problem should be handled by the after-sales service team and the product availability question by the sales team. In the sales scenario, I would suggest that social media has served as a *lead generator*, with the social media content prompting the consumer to contact the organization.

However, this transfer of the consumer from one element of marketing (social media) to another (sales or service and support) is where problems frequently exist. There should be no difficulty in applying this kind of joined-up thinking, but sadly, the joined-up organization rarely exists. The problem? Twenty years in and *digital* is still too often seen as a separate entity to other aspects of marketing. One of the biggest problems I come across in larger organizations, particularly B2B, is the disconnection between the web presence and the sales team.

A key problem of *dark* social is, therefore, that the social team has to justify its existence and budget, so want to hold onto contacts made on a social media platform when realistically their job has been done in initiating the contact. If what constitutes *dark* social (i.e., personal contact) is kept within the social media remit then the customer slips off the digital radar. Take, for example, a social media-originated message that is copied or attached to an e-mail—there is no digital record (footprint) of that message being disseminated beyond its original publication. This is unlike, for example, a click on a link on social media to the brand website. It is worth a quick reminder here that—perhaps for the aforementioned social media marketers who know little outside their domain—e-mail is still the most used platform on the Internet. Indeed, Gmail alone is used more than *all* social media put together. In comparison, social media is very much the new kid on the block making a lot of noise to be noticed. Note: see title of this book.

However, it only gets worse for marketers in that e-mail is not the only element of *dark* social in that messaging apps on the likes of WhatsApp,

WeChat, and Facebook Messenger are all one-to-one forms of digital communication. Note also that Facebook and Linkedin offer "unpublished posts," which are promoted and targeted posts that are not published on the brand page—these are also sometimes described as being part of *dark* social.

A postscript to this would be that social media marketing is generally recognized as being a method of encouraging *engagement* by the customer with the organization, brand, or product that is conducted in a public environment. If that same objective is sought via direct communication with individuals it has existed as the concept of *relationship marketing* for quite some time. However, some of us sales and marketing old timers consider that relationship marketing is little more than what we used to call *good* customer service. Again, specialist digital marketers take note.

## 3.3 Models Associated With Social Media Marketing

Having addressed the issue of what isn't social media marketing, there are a number of concepts that are very closely associated with social media marketing, but are not part of social media marketing as such. However, it is important that these models are understood before any attempt at social media marketing is considered.

### 3.3.1 Viral Marketing

Prior to the Internet and social media, viral marketing was known as word-of-mouth marketing. However, as seems the case in so many aspects of digital marketing, a word of explanation is required before the subject is investigated any further. *Word-of-mouth* is: "an oral, person-to-person communication between a receiver and a communicator (whom the receiver perceives as a non-commercial) regarding a brand, a product or a service" (Arndt 1967). In other words, it is customers passing on their opinion about a product, brand, or organization because they are impressed by it. That these discussions often took place in its vicinity, this was often called *water cooler talk*—who hasn't recommended a movie or retail outlet in such circumstances? And how many people heard of the

Atkin's Diet in this way—a product that lent itself to self-propagation if ever there was one. With the advent of the Internet the water cooler became merely a place to get a drink, e-mail and then social media taking its place. No longer did movie goers tell a couple of people their views on a movie, they could tell dozens, hundreds, even thousands at the click of a mouse or touch of a screen. A final point on the issue of the *digital* viral story is that those that have gone most viral (I hate to think what my old English teacher at grammar school would have to say about how I now use the word viral) have had a nonviral boost from a broadcast media. There is nothing like a humorous cell phone video of a man chasing his dog through a park shouting its name to end a news bulletin[2] and that will reach a whole new audience who will in turn reach for their mobile device and immediately look it up (research suggests most people watch TV and look at another screen at the same time). A mention in a newspaper has just the same effect.

Word-of-mouth *marketing*, on the other hand, involves the marketer putting out a marketing message and then encouraging—or *persuading*—people to pass that message on to other people, preferably who will be potential customers for the product, brand, or organization. Importantly, customers might be offered an inducement to spread the word. For example: free or discounted products if *friends* are introduced to a product that they subsequently purchase—Uber has used this tactic extensively. Indeed, using the taxi company as an example: if a colleague told you that they had used Uber and they were impressed with the service, that would be *word-of-mouth*. If that colleague forwarded Uber's pre-formed text to you and you got a $10 discount on your first journey, that would be word-of-mouth *marketing*.

Furthermore, there is the issue of the term *viral* in this context. Viral and viruses in nature have existed, well… forever. In the digital age, however, the terms have become associated with something—usually malevolent—that spreads quickly and easily from one computer to another. It was inevitable, therefore, that when digital technology (predominantly by way of e-mail) enabled people to send the same message to tens/hundreds/

---

[2] As did the BBC in the case of Fenton the Labrador (look it up on a search engine of your choice).

thousands of their friends and associates with the click of a mouse that it became known as the message *going viral*. These viral messages were usually entertaining in some way, hence the legend of the cute cat and skateboarding dog. Jokes too got around at alarming speed. Not social media as such, but closely related, is that in the early days of e-mail I spent a lot of time advising organizations on a staff protocol for sending and receiving e-mails on the company domain name e-mail server. One of the serious issues was staff receiving viral jokes that were of a sexual, racial, or otherwise offensive nature—which then frequently found their way into the in-boxes of other staff who were rightly offended. Does that sound familiar to organization's social media protocols being developed now? Or perhaps more relevantly; those social media protocols that should be, but are not being, developed.

Viral marketing, described as "network-enhanced word-of-mouth" by the venture capitalist behind Hotmail, Steve Jurvetson—who is commonly attributed with being the first to use the term—is the practice of marketers deliberately developing a marketing message that will go *digitally* viral around potential customers. That marketers hoped that the message, whatever it might be, would create a *buzz* among the public resulted in the procedure also being known as buzz marketing. In keeping with other aspects of social media marketing covered in this book, however, given the nature of the message in many viral campaigns, perhaps viral *advertising* better suits the practice.

It is also impossible to emphasize enough that, to be successful, viral marketing campaigns must be strategically planned and executed, they do not *just happen*. Furthermore, many campaigns that are strategically planned and executed fail to go viral—we only hear of the ones that do.

However, I would contest that *pure* marketing viral is a fiction. In the UK, upon winning a top business award, Sarah Wood, founder of tech firm Unruly, was asked in a BBC radio interview: "what does Unruly do?" and she replied: "We help videos go viral." Yes, for the uninitiated, commercial *virals* don't just happen—though cute cats and skateboarding dogs might. There was even a live video feed of a puddle in a city near me last year that, it seems, was watched by most people in the known universe. Maybe back in 2007 Ms Wood read an excellent article in Techcrunch.

com and was inspired to set up her business. I've been pointing skeptical students at it for the last 10 years. It is called *The Secret Strategies Behind Many Viral Videos*. Just put that into a search engine and have a read. If you are not aware of this stuff it is a real eye-opener.

I trust that by now it is obvious that the contemporary viral marketing campaign depends on social media to succeed—hence its inclusion in this chapter.

### 3.3.2 Influencers

In any society there has always existed (and always will exist) a very small number of people who will be advocates—evangelists even—of any product, brand, or organization. These folk wield a significant influence over the buying decisions of people who seek advice, guidance, or recommendation on particular products, brands, or organizations. Those from whom such advice is sought are identified by marketers as being *influencers*.

In the previous chapter, Nielsen's 90-9-1 rule introduced us to the notion that the majority of social media content is produced by a small number of people but read by a large number of people. Human nature is such that people who like to express their positive opinions on organizations, brands, or products are drawn to new media in order for their viewpoint to reach a wider audience. Ergo, we have the social media *influencers* (sometimes called *e-fluencers*).

As with other elements within this book, the *social* aspects came first. Advocates and evangelists tend to act in an altruistic manner offering their opinion for no fiscal recompense—that they gain notoriety is generally their reward. However, at the same time as those cunning digital marketers came to realize that *some* social media writers were open to making a profit from their proclamations, *some* influencers became more mercenary, seeking rewards that are financial than philanthropic. Although programmatic advertising already allowed the social media influencers to make money by selling advertising space around their content, being offered cash or products to endorse those products increased their bank balance more efficiently.

However, this is yet another traditional marketing tactic that seems to have been (re)-invented by social media marketing *experts* whereas in reality the practice goes back as far as mankind has traded (give silk to an influential dress designer and soon everyone wants clothes made from the silk you sell). The concept was *formalized* as such by Katz and Lazarfeld in 1955—though the latter had proposed the concept some 10 years earlier. Problematically, traditional—that is, offline—influencers were always hard for marketers to identify. Online, not only is the opposite true, but marketers can use digital technology to assess influencers' power by monitoring the blogs, reviews, social media content, and websites created by these online brand advocates. Furthermore, where offline influencers were normally personalities in TV, radio, and print—making them a kind of elite—digital influencers, as Chris Anderson points out in his seminal book *The Long Tail* (2006), "aren't a super-elite of people cooler than us; they are us." This aspect of "are us" is perhaps behind findings in a study by Markerly Inc. (2016) which suggest that—on Instagram, at least—as an influencer's follower total rises, the rate of engagement (likes and comments) with followers decreases, with 1K to 10K followers seeming to be the optimum. As follow counts rise, it seems the super-influencers are considered to be *less* like us?

The news for marketers is not all good, however. Influencers have expectations—or is that *demands*—with many social media influencers seeing their role as being professional rather than amateur. However, in the great scheme of things that is strategic marketing, the sums paid to bloggers who will reach a specific targeted audience in a voice they will respond to is negligible compared to other marketing activities. These fees—usually negotiated by agents and dependent on the number of readers, followers, or friends the influencer has—have prompted the public (and some social media content writers) to see any *inducements* as little more than bribery for publicity. Figure 3.1 shows the results of research by Roy (2014) which suggests what influencers expect in return for endorsing an organization, brand, or product.

Indeed, from a marketing standpoint many endorsements are little more than adverts—something with which the *Federal Trade Commission* (*FTC*) has a tendency to agree (note that there are legal issues with regard to the payment of influencers, these are addressed in Chapter 4 (Section

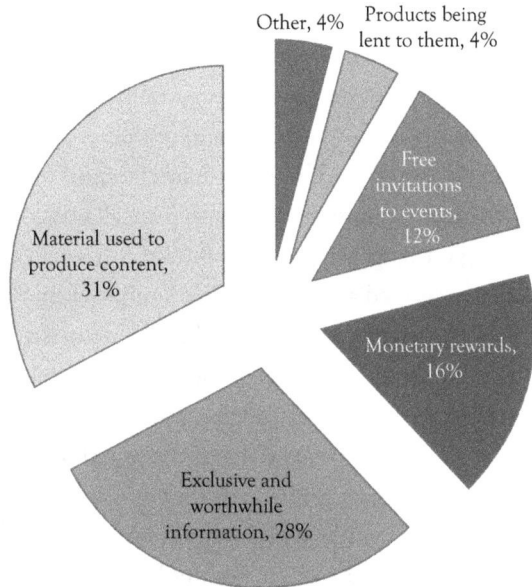

*Figure 3.1  Influencer expectations*

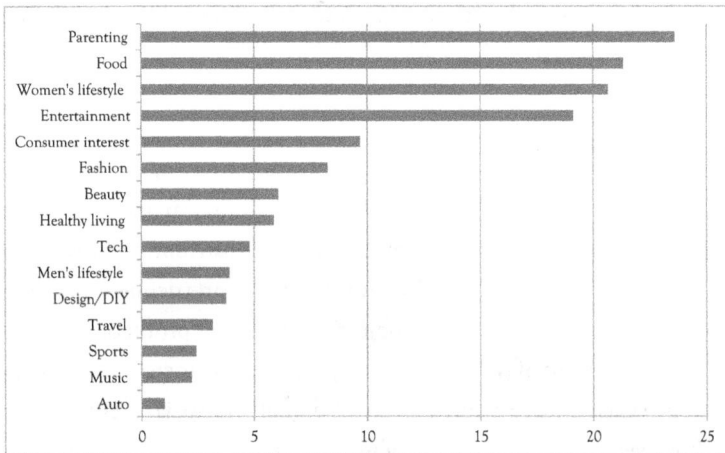

*Figure 3.2  Subject popularity among advocate bloggers*

4.5)). That the social media marketer has little control over the influencer's output, the brand might find itself being cited by the FTC because the influencer has broken the rules.

Furthermore, as is the case with all social media marketing, calculating return on investment can be difficult—*engagement* does not necessarily translate into purchases. There is also the issue of the quality of the influencer's followers; are they *real* or the product of an astute—or dubious—recruitment strategy? Finally, influencers can go from hero to zero overnight (see the example of PewDiePie in the upcoming section on blogging) and, even if the brand can extract itself from the misdemeanors of an influencer, the time and resources put into the relationship are all wasted.

Concentrating on blogs written by influencers (though they use the term *advocates*), social media marketing solution provider SocialChorus (2014) identified the relative popularity of blog subjects (see Figure 3.2). Note that there is a crossover within some of the verticals—hence the percentage shown amounts to over 100 percent.

SocialChorus also makes the case that if the brand or organization is looking to work with bloggers as advocates then crossovers should be used to their advantage. For example, if you want to work with food bloggers, it would also be advisable to contact healthy living bloggers, consumer interest bloggers, and parenting bloggers for spreading associated marketing messages (Charlesworth 2015). A further observation of these figures would be to suggest that these figures for blogging subjects might well translate to *all* social media. Perhaps not exactly—but pretty close.

### 3.3.3 Content Marketing

Defined by the Content Marketing Institute (contentmarketinginstitute.com) as "A marketing technique of creating and distributing relevant and valuable content to attract, acquire, and engage a clearly defined and understood target audience—with the objective of driving profitable customer action," the concept of *content* marketing has become increasingly popular in recent years. Like so many aspects of digital and social media marketing, however, no one seems to be absolutely sure what it is. Certainly the model of creating *useful* content to attract potential customers is not new, but the digital age has moved things along somewhat—not least because it is attractive to the search engine algorithms that have placed an emphasis on the quality of online content. Robert Rose, the chief strategy officer of the aforementioned Content Marketing Institute, gives a more pragmatic clue to what it is in his definition: "Traditional marketing and advertising is *telling* the world you're a rock star. Content Marketing is *showing* the world that you are one." Perhaps a little more helpful is the definition of Heidi Cohen, chief content officer, Actionable Marketing Guide, who says: "Content Marketing provides consumers with useful information to aid purchase decisions, improve product usage and entertain them while achieving organizational goals without being overtly promotional." So we kind-of know what content marketing is, and we know the media formats in which it can be published, that is: social media, blogs, articles, white papers, case studies, research reports, guides, webinars, shared documents, podcasts, Q+A pages, videos, forums, and infographics, but clearly there is still the problem of no one seeming to know—or at least they won't tell us—what *content* is.

To help, let's go back to the Content Marketing Institute's definition, which suggests the content be: "relevant and valuable content to attract, acquire, and engage a clearly defined and understood target audience— with the objective of driving profitable customer action." Well, that seems to suggest that the content of *content* marketing is anything the marketer wants it to be. Or should that be: anything *the customer needs* it to be. That being the case, content is different for every organization, brand, or product and the different markets or market segments that might buy the product. It would seem that developing content for content marketing is not as simple as it may seem. At this point I will direct you to Chapter 5 (Section 5.1), where the issue of appointing the *right* staff is addressed. I will conclude with one tip that is pretty much universally accepted. Content must *not* be sales copy. For example: "our widget is the greatest widget in the world and it will more than match the performance of our competitors. Buy it now and get the accessory pack free" is not the *content* of content marketing.

### 3.3.4 Paid, Owned, and Earned Media

A concept popular in digital marketing whose popularity is as a result of the impact of social media is that of *Paid*, *Owned*, and *Earned* media. Like many concepts, the practice has existed for as long as mankind has traded goods for reward, but it is only recently that it has been given a name—and it is one that has its roots in the non-marketing marketer phenomenon in that it is heavily dependent on technologists and automation. Many argue that its swift rise to prominence is being followed by an equally swift decline—indeed, this could well be yet another of those concepts that look good in theory but are rarely used in practice—and when they are, it is as a guide rather than strategic tool. The three elements are:

- **Paid** (also known as bought). Marketing in any media where the promotion is paid for by the selling organization. Effectively, this is advertising on any media including TV, print, and the Internet as well as direct mail.
- **Owned**. Any media where the product, brand, or organization has control over that media and/or the content in it. This includes such things as brochures, retail outlets, websites, and—to a limited degree because the platform is not owned—social media marketing sites such as Facebook.
- **Earned**. The product, brand, or organization is deemed worthy of custom and/or loyalty from consumers based on the organization's way of doing business (e.g., offering excellent service as the norm) which generates consumer-generated content in social media—the reason the concept is prominent in digital marketing.

Perhaps in an attempt to revive an ailing patient, some commentators have added a fourth component; *shared*. However, this refers predominantly to social media shares, and so is seen by many as an extension of either *owned* (a post by the organization is *shared* by users of the platform) or *earned* (a complimentary post by a customer is shared with other users).

### 3.3.5 Blogging

Although both the popular and trade press consistently refer to the likes of Facebook and Twitter when extolling the virtues of social media marketing, it is blogging that can get the marketing message across more effectively. As Brown and Fiorella say in their book *Influence Marketing* (2013): "blogging offers the medium where a brand can be truly itself and offer the exact messaging for which it wants to be recognized and respected." A more forceful endorsement for blogs over other social media platforms comes from digital marketing maven Debbie Weil (2009). She says: "Corporate blogs are your digital hub—the home base or mother ship for all your social networking and online communications." She also emphasizes that "As seductive as Twitter and Facebook are for instant communication, you don't control the service ... they own the platforms," a point I make rather forcefully in Chapter 5 (Section 5.3)—that the section is titled *my house my rules* should give you the gist of how much I agree with Ms Weil's statement. I also agree with her when she says that people "should not get hung on the word blog," suggesting that *social site* as a better term. I often ponder that the present generation of *wonder kinder* social media marketers eschew blogs simply because the term comes from the previous century and so is not *hip* enough for them? And finally, if you doubt her credentials for making such statements, just type "Debbie Weil" into Google (or any other search engine—they do exist apparently).

Common versions of commercial blogs include the following:

- The company evangelist: a less formal presentation than corporate literature or even website, this suits organizations where a culture of staff participation and involvement is paramount. The passion of the writer plays a big part in imbuing a feel-good enthusiasm to the reader. The blog could be used to talk about new products, uses for existing ones, or problem solving.
- The product blog: although this can become more akin to an online community, such a blog can lead the conversation about product uses and attributes whilst still allowing users to respond via the feedback facility.
- The CEO/director blog: more formal than the company evangelist, but still comparatively informal, this is perhaps the most difficult to get right. Success or failure is often down to the personality of the writer. Ghost writers can be used—but these are easily uncovered if the content doesn't ring true.
- The event blog: these are not permanent, but are used in the run-up to, or during an event or as part of a wider promotional strategy.

- Press releases: any blog might include these as a quick, and relatively inexpensive, way of making news available to both the general public and media professionals. However, care should be taken to ensure the PR fits with the nature of the blog content.
- The promotional blog: this is the kind of blog written by small-business owners or managers. Popular at one time, social media platforms such as Facebook have replaced many of them—although they can still be used to promote the writer's expertise in the industry or market.

As will be made clear in later subsequent chapters, it is the nature of the industry, market, product, and—most importantly—the *culture* of the organization that will ultimately dictate how appropriate it is for the organization to include a blog as part of its digital marketing.

A recurring theme throughout the rest of the book is that like all communication that represents the organization, brand, or product its content must be considered carefully, as does the issue of who will develop and write that content. For the commercial organization, a blog would be a permanent, almost full-time, job for a member of staff, plus backup to cover holidays, illness, and so on. In some organizations, outsourcing the blog to a professional or agency might be the best option. Leaving the global reputation of the organization to an unskilled member of staff is not good practice. For *not good practice*, read: potential social media disaster.

### 3.3.6 Consumer Reviews and Feedback

I frequently put forward an argument that the most significant impact that the Internet has had on both consumers and sellers is in the way in which it enables the general public to present the world with their own comments about products and services they have purchased or experienced. I also make the same argument that other aspects of the Internet should not belittle the role consumer reviews have played in changing the way businesses function and their attitude toward meeting the needs of their customers. I would certainly argue that, of all the elements of social media marketing, reviews have had the biggest impact—definitely more than the press's darlings: Facebook and Twitter. Naturally, this means I wholeheartedly concur with Andrew Keen, when he suggests in his book *The Cult of the Amateur* (2007) that the ability of the buying public to reach such a large audience presented a "real and present danger" to the established business culture.

It is important to differentiate between the general public giving their review of a product and the role of marketers in the subject of customer reviews. One discussion I frequently have with my digitally obsessed students is that if a company offers customers the product they need, in a place they need it, at a price that is agreeable to them; and this after making the customer aware of the product and its price in a timely fashion, then customer reviews are nothing to worry about as—if any are given—they will always be positive.

Just in case you missed it, I said that if you get the marketing mix (the 4Ps) right, you'll do alright in business. OK, so that's rather simplistic, but then marketers do have a habit of making simple things complicated. If nothing else—as I alluded to earlier—the *fear* of bad reviews has prompted (forced?) businesses to improve their product or service offerings, which means getting the 4Ps *right*.

That customer-generated reviews impact on fellow consumers in their buying process has been proved beyond reasonable doubt, with buyers trusting consumer reviews more than professional reviews, which are perceived as being part of the marketing of the product. This trust of *people like me* is based on the psychological phenomenon (mentioned in the previous chapter) of social proof. The concept suggests that people look to what others are doing for reassurance—the assumption being that others possess more knowledge or are better informed than they are. As is my wont, I'll throw in a caveat that will become more common, and with more emphasis, as the pages go by. That caveat is this. We do not seek help, reassurance—call it what you will—for every product we buy. Indeed, if the calculation was based purely on the *quantity* of our purchases we seek reviews on a very small proportion of what we buy. Disagree? Try compiling a list of your purchases for the last week. Then cross out those you purchased without referring to a review. You should have deleted pretty much everything us marketers call convenience (or shopping) products.

That's *probably* just about everything under, let's say $5. Possibly $10? Possibly $20? Indeed, the cost of goods plays a big part in whether we seek the advice of others or not. The higher the price, the more research we do. But then that's not exactly rocket science is it? And yes, I do appreciate we can all (a) spend an inordinate amount of time deciding on whether or not to by something for less than a dollar (a pound in my case), or (b) buy expensive products with the heart not the brain that is made without due care and consideration (at least one car in my case). However, this section is on the use of reviews, not buyer behavior per se.

On the issue of who writes reviews I'll remind you of Nielsen's 90-9-1 rule (again). Perhaps the proliferation of opportunities to leave reviews has moved the "1" up a bit, but it is still a minority of buyers who leave reviews. Note that for the sake of this book, I am invoking the grammatical difference between *reviews* and *feedback*. Although related, feedback is far less critical or thorough. As an example: we've all simply ticked the feedback boxes on eBay (haven't we?) but that is not a *review* of either the seller's service or the product. Indeed, how many of us have ever completed an eBay or Amazon product review? Not me.

So why—or when—do we leave reviews? Contemporary thinking, supported by psychological research, is that review writers are predominantly motivated by goodwill and positive sentiment, that is; when we are very happy with our purchase. Conversely, extreme disappointment of a product or service might also prompt us to take some of our own time to make a comment. Interestingly, positive comments are generally written as a *thank you* to the seller and negative comments as a *warning* to potential buyers. Persuasion to write a review can also be affected by (a) our level of commitment to the product, brand, or organization—we *thank* those we feel we have a relationship with, (b) our expectations of the purchase—reviews on expensive products are often nitpicky, (c) the price of the goods—I ignored the request for feedback on a 75 pence/cent household bulb I had purchased, and (d) what's to review—I was recently asked to review the car park I used at a local airport; "I arrived, I parked, I left."

For marketers, options for the use of consumer reviews boil down to (a) hosting reviews on the organization's own web presence—normally its website—and responding to them or (b) taking advantage of reviews on other sites. The obvious difference is that in the former the organization has control over any comments while on the latter it has little or none. For the reviews that are on a web presence controlled by the organization there has to be an emphasis on encouraging users to add to the reviews—hopefully good ones (see previous comments regarding getting the marketing mix right).

Indeed, it might be argued that the key role for the digital marketers in consumer reviews is to encourage customers to actually leave comments or feedback on a review facility. Service providers such as restaurants have any obvious advantage in that there is personal interaction between all customers and staff and so verbal request can be made. Other businesses do not have the same customer contact and so any personal appeal to them must be deliberate and planned. The obvious problem being that if the customer feels that a request for their feedback is insistent, intrusive, or simply too overt, then the result is the opposite of the desired effect. Adopting a phrase that dates back to the early western movies where the good guys wore white hats and the bad guys black hats (and commonly used in search engine optimization) there are *white hat* methods of collecting reviews and those that are black hat. And there are some that are somewhere in-between, though I can't remember cowboys ever wearing *gray* hats.

| | |
|---|---|
| | Top of the *black hat* tactics is offering any kind of payment for a positive review—this could be by way of straight cash, or a discount on a product or service. |
| | Offering *free* gifts might encourage customers to leave a review—but the gift may well tilt them toward that review being positive. Similarly, friends and family are easy to communicate with to request reviews—but they are hardly likely to give a bad one. I think you can probably guess that this is considered a black hat area by some folk. |
| | Asking customers for genuine reviews—this could be via e-mail, social media, printed leaflets, or facilities at the point of sale or service. Of course, you could ask face-to-face, but hovering over a customer as they write a review would move the request into the gray category as few folks will criticize people face-to-face. |

(Charlesworth 2015).

A final section on this subject is that of readers' comments on social media pages. I have included it here but it could be in a number of sections in a number of chapters, not least in Chapter 5 (Section 5.3) that considers the control social media platforms have over its users. This chapter is on social media marketing, but there is a crossover with the use of societal social media. If we start with the latter, it has become common for users to leave comments that are either (a) not connected with the subject of the post, (b) abusive, (c) a combination of the two, or (d) an advert for themselves or something that they will benefit from the sale of. For examples of (a), (b), and (c) pick any music track you wish, search for it on YouTube and while the video is playing read the comments beneath it. Quite why anyone who abuses another who has given positive comments about the song is on the page in the first place is a bit of a mystery—simply the opportunity to abuse *anyone* for *anything* has to be a possibility. But the comments go off on tangents to the tune and its performers. Just about any song from 1963 to 1974 has the potential to attract Vietnam War comments, for example, which will extend into the Gulf Wars, which in turn tend to attract racial comments. Reading such threads is not a pleasant experience. In 2009, writing for the UK's *Guardian* newspaper, journalists Paul Owen and Christopher Wright described this kind of user comments as:

> Juvenile, aggressive, misspelled, sexist, homophobic, swinging from raging at the contents of a video to providing a pointlessly detailed description followed by a LOL, YouTube comments are a hotbed of infantile debate and unashamed ignorance—with the occasional burst of wit shining through.

The *advert* comments (with an outgoing link) can be posted individually by users, but are more likely to be automated. I suspect you've all seen them; they are usually telling you that you could earn a zillion dollars an hour doing something or other that requires no skill whatsoever.

Certainly, trolls exist on personal sites, but of more relevance to social media marketers is this type of comments when left on *commercial* pages. In this instance I am considering the social media content of individuals who are also brands where their social media comments are part of maintaining their brand awareness in the marketplace—even if they are noncommercial in nature, that is: "I've just had a shower" rather than "my new album is on sale next week." There have been a number of high-profile exits from social media, with celebrity-for-many-reasons Stephen Fry being one. Far, far more eloquent than me, I'll let Mr Fry tell why he quit Twitter in 2016.

> Oh goodness, what fun twitter was in the early days, a secret bathing-pool in a magical glade in an enchanted forest. It was glorious "to turn as swimmers into cleanness leaping." We frolicked and water-bombed and sometimes, in the moonlight, skinny-dipped. We chattered and laughed and put the world to rights and shared thoughts sacred, silly and profane. But now the pool is stagnant. It is frothy with scum, clogged with weeds and littered with broken glass, sharp rocks and slimy rubbish.

> To leave that metaphor, let us grieve at what twitter has become. A stalking ground for the sanctimoniously self-righteous who love to second-guess, to leap to conclusions and be offended—worse, to be offended on behalf of others they do not even know.

Even Swedish gamer Felix "PewDiePie" Kjellberg, who is famous only for being a superstar YouTuber with more than 30 million subscribers, told his followers—the *Bro Army*—in 2014 that he had disabled comments on his channel because they were "mainly spam, it's people self-advertising, it's people trying to provoke." Perhaps it was all part of his own self-marketing, but comments and actions by the people who were— effectively—YouTube's bread and butter prompted the video platform to address this issue (Mr. Kjellberg pushed his luck too far early in 2017, with his series of anti-Semitic comments resulting him being dropped by Disney and having YouTube pull his channel from its *Google Preferred* advertising). Which segues nicely into the reason this subject is in this chapter. January 2017 saw YouTube introduce a new source of income for creators (and so, YouTube also), a service dubbed *Super Chat*, which let fans pay to have their comments *pinned* to the top of YouTuber livestreams. I feel *brand posters* such as the aforementioned Mr PewDiePie might see this as an ill-disguised inducement to keep their comments section enabled. Or should social media marketers simply see this as another way to get those millionaire-in-a-day ads in front of gullible members of the population? I struggle to see any value in *legitimate* marketers using such tactics. Indeed, I wonder if *Super Chat* still exists by the time you are reading this.

### 3.3.7 Social Networking and Online Communities

Apology: throughout this section I refer to Facebook as an example. Yes, I know there are other network and community platforms out there, but Facebook is the market leader and I cannot believe that anyone reading this book has not only heard of Facebook, but is aware of how it functions.

As I promised when it was first mentioned in Chapter 1, it is relevant at this point to remind you that Facebook is (a) not part of social media, it is an entity that exists to *facilitate* social media, and (b) it exists to make money for its owners and shareholders. The same goes for all social media platforms.

Nonetheless, any marketer or business person would doff their metaphorical cap at the way in which the likes of Facebook and LinkedIn have developed their product offering (the provision of web space to be used by *members*) to such an extent that they dominate the industry in such a way that organizations feel they must not only use their services, but advertise that service on the organization's own products, stationery, vehicles, and websites. Kudos to them for that. Indeed, such is the dominant nature of Facebook that some customers would rather visit the web presence of an organization, brand, or product on a third-party platform than on the website of that organization, brand, or product. Furthermore, the organization, brand, or product chooses to use that third-party platform—over which it has no control—to its own online domain. This is not, of course, totally its own choice. That so many of their customers and potential customers have free access to Facebook is a far more attractive proposition than the effort, resources, and money it takes to attract that number of people to its own website. Indeed, the likes of Wal-Mart with its *Hub*, Anheuser-Busch's *Bud.tv*, and KLM/Air France with their *Bluenity.com* are examples of high-profile brands that failed with their own domain social network sites. However, this is not an absolute and it is likely that as Facebook—and others—change the terms and conditions of use of their platforms, brands will be tempted to move their social media to sites that they own. Note that we will return to this notion later in the book.

So what do social networking and online communities offer marketers? In a nutshell; access to highly segmented customers and a natural platform for interactive promotions and the opportunity to actively engage with their customers that was simply not available to them prior to the Internet in general and social media specifically. John Battelle made this point in his influential—and best-selling—book, *Search* (2005), saying: "the very idea that our relationships with others (our social network) or our relationships to goods and services (our commercial network) were anything but ephemeral was presumed: without the internet, how could it be otherwise?"

Essentially, the social media marketer has two choices in deciding how to use networks and communities as part of any marketing strategy. The first is to use them as a channel for the dissemination of a marketing message—albeit a message that is disguised as engagement with the customer. Wait; *disguised*? Yes folks, relationship marketing is a form of marketing. Are you seriously suggesting that employees of an organization would really want a relationship with their customers if it wasn't part of their job? And—ultimately—their job is to make money for their employers. OK, so there might be some businesses out there that are truly altruistic—but check them out in a couple of years and see if they are still trading. What about not-for-profits? I hear you ask. Well, yes … to a degree. But *not-for-profit* means no profit to give to shareholders, it does not mean *at a loss*. The second way in which marketers can use networks and communities is as an aspect of customer care and support. This is covered in more detail later in the chapter.

One thing networks and communities—and probably all aspects of social media—cannot provide the marketer with is *new* customers, that is; people do not discover the organization, brand, or product on social media having never heard of it before. Remember, this book is on social media marketing, *not* social media. Certainly, friends might post on their Facebook page that they have bought a new product, it is wonderful, and everyone should buy it, but that is social conversation, it is chitchat, it is water cooler talk … it is not marketing.

Social media is most effective for (a) retaining existing customers by developing and maintaining a relationship, or (b) helping potential new customers as they work their way down the buying funnel of their purchase decision making having been made aware of the organization, brand, or product somewhere else. It is very rare—and then probably by chance—that a potential buyer discovers an organization, brand, or product via its social media presence. Need an example? It is almost certain that before you signed up for your present (and/or past) university or college you will have accessed its *official* social media presences (there will be other student-developed pages). However, that will be *after* you have become aware of that university, be that via its marketing, its reputation (marketers would argue reputation = brand = marketing), its prospectus (marketing again), a family member, a friend, or a former tutor or your school or college careers department. A caveat to this (a polite way of saying *cover my back*) is that Facebook would like Facebook to become everyone's gateway to the Internet, part of this being that search engines will be replaced by a search on Facebook for whatever it is you are looking for. Such is the power of Google—and our routine use of search engines—I cannot see that happening, but hey, you never know; we got Brexit and Trump.

For developing and maintaining a relationship you could do worse than following the advice given by Facebook itself. The *Facebook for Business* website (facebook.com/business) suggests that organizations:

- Be responsive.
- Be consistent.
- Do what works.
- Make successful posts into successful promotions.

As we will see in subsequent chapters, it's not quite as easy as Facebook would like us to think—neither does it suggest what organizations should *not* do. I would suggest that social media is *not* a place for comments when:

- The product, brand, or organization is only talking about itself.
- The post is there to meet a quota or predetermined target.

- Replies or reactions are not monitored.
- There is a perceived obligation to post—comments should be posted for a reason, not to feed a habit.

But most important of all:

- They are not genuine.

(Charlesworth 2015)

For helping potential new customers in their purchase decision there are three ways the organization, brand, or product's network or community social media presence might influence their decision. These are:

1. Provide information that might sway a choice (the product is bigger, faster, etc. than rivals). However, this kind of information is normally sought on manufacturers' or retailers' websites.
2. By the nature, culture, and ethos of the presented content the buyer is encouraged to feel an affinity to the product, brand, or organization.
3. The input of the *followers* is so positive that it encourages purchase.

Network or community campaigns, however, do not have to be focused on the product, brand, or organization. Procter & Gamble, for example, has developed social media campaigns around personal issues that are important to the consumers that the organization wished to engage with—bullying of teenage girls, for example. Similarly, Unilever used social media to encourage women to question their negative perception of their own looks. Again, as a marketer, I recognize the excellence of these campaigns and real-life issues they address—but the campaigns were not wholly altruistic; they encouraged sales of *Secret* deodorant and *Dove* soap respectively. Both also used other media extensively—see my early comments on when is social media marketing *not* social media marketing.

### 3.3.8 Social Sharing

I have to start this section with another apology; basically, this is the same apology as at the beginning of the previous section—except for this section:

replace *Facebook* with *Twitter* for text messages, *Instagram* for images, and *YouTube* for videos. An addendum to this is to mention that Instagram is owned by Facebook, and YouTube by Google. It's a *small* digital world.

As with the networking aspects of social media covered in the previous chapter, defining the various elements of social media is far from being an exact science and so it is for social *sharing*. Indeed, although I use Twitter as a mainstay of this chapter, there is a reasonable argument for it being in the previous one. Moreover, given that it is sometimes described as a microblogging site, it could also have been addressed in the earlier section on that subject. However, I think that description is nebulous; 140 characters (or 280 as it is now) is not sufficient for a true blogger to express their ideas and opinions fully—only a snapshot of them. Social media marketers should be aware that the classifications I have settled on should be considered imprecise—and all aspects of social networking and sharing *could* and *should* be considered interchangeable (Charlesworth 2015).

That social sharing is commonly described as the *broadcasting of our thoughts and activities* immediately gives rise to the notion that the medium not only has potential as a marketing tool, but that it is closer to traditional marketing than other social media platforms. In a way this is correct as it encourages the sending of brief messages without the engagement expected of networks and communities.

Social sharing can be divided into three different—though related—parts: messages that are textual, those that are images, and those that are in video format. Before considering each in turn, however, there are a number of caveats that pervade all three, and they are:

- Any message sent should not be overtly *marketing*, social media participants do not like to be lied to, or even fooled. They don't even like to be marketed at (Charlesworth 2014).
- Every message must be perceived by the receiver as valuable; if it isn't, they won't read it. Similarly, quality always trumps quantity.
- In the previous chapter, mention is made of many messages being sent on social media, but relatively few being read. This must be factored in to any expected return on investment for a social sharing campaign.

### Textual Messages

Although images and videos can also be sent on the platform, text messages are Twitter's bread and butter. The simplicity of the (original) 140-character message might almost be considered to have been designed for marketers rather than the social use for which it was intended. After all, sales and marketing copywriters have been used to writing to similar constraints for decades. Social sharing also offers marketers immediacy—switched-on social media marketing can react to world events as they happen, though often badly (examples of the good and the embarrassing are included in Chapter 6). From a marketing perspective then, Twitter can be seen as being *instant*, whereas social networks are more akin to *conversations*, communities about *engaging*. Tweets can be used to inform customers of any news, event, product, promotion, or special offer that is appropriate to the sender and its Twitter audience. However, it is the informality of Twitter—140 characters lends itself to abbreviations and *text-speak*—that is; at the core of its benefit to marketers, allowing them to be perceived as real people rather than faceless brands, products, or organizations.

### Image Messages

As with their textual cousins, image-based social media platforms such as Instagram allow marketers to target specific groups of users with their marketing message. Individuals effectively segment themselves by the photos they keep, send, resend, and comment on. Pictures lend themselves to certain markets and industries, with retailers benefitting most. It is also easier to send a picture that is not overtly marketing. For example, a fashion retailer could send an image of a new dress to their target segment with the message: "here's part of our new range … how good would you look in this?" Sales copy would be: "here's part of our new range … buy now for free shipping."

### Video Messages

Although Facebook is closing fast—or has already past, depending on which reports you read—YouTube is the main player in social video. Yet again, however, it is important to appreciate that YouTube was set up to show homemade, social videos—the classic dog-on-a-skateboard type of thing. However, rather like eBay's move from yard sale to host for shops, YouTube is now predominantly the home of professional videos, be they of pop music, clips from movies and TV shows (or entire shows), or adverts shown on—and made for—TV.

As with all social media platforms, users can develop their own space on YouTube where they can post their own videos as well as a selection of the favorites from other sources so that friends can see them. For the organization, brand, or product there is the *YouTube One Channel* where their own videos can be posted and made available—an additional bonus is that these videos can be embedded on their own website.

Although amateur handheld-camera videos can work for some products or brands, organizations are best advised to use only professional content on YouTube. You might even be surprised at how many of the *amateur* videos are actually staged by professional film crews because the effect is deemed more appealing for social media. Oh those marketers—they're a tricky bunch.

### 3.3.9 Social Service and Support

If it isn't a statement of the glaringly obvious, this subject refers to the use of social media as a medium for providing service and/or support to customers. Pretty much by definition, this means some kind of after-sales service, and not part of any pre-sales marketing effort—though evidence of such service may have some bearing on a customer's purchase behavior.

Such service is successfully practiced by relatively few organizations. This state of affairs may well change in the near future as service and support on social media is now expected by some customers or market segments—in particular the generation that has grown up with the Internet who now considers digital to be the norm.

Social service and support can be broken into two facets: *proactive* and *reactive*.

Proactive Service and Support

This is where online communities and/or social networks are used as part of the overall package of product or service offered to the customer when they make a purchase with a concentration being on improving the customer *experience* and so their use or enjoyment of the purchased product is enhanced by this service. The nature of this service lends itself to being conducted in public, where the customers and potential customers can see the good work of the organization.

Reactive Service and Support

As it concentrates on being reactive to events that are normally—almost by definition—negative, this element might be better described as *after-sales* service and support and is provided as a response to customers' requests, queries, or complaints. Essentially, this means that the customer experience (the proactive aspect of service and support) has failed and so the customer is coming to the organization via social media for support, or more likely, help, recompense, or to complain. For this reason it is a reasonable argument that interactions with disgruntled customers should be conducted out of the public eye that is social media.

There is a third option for social service and support that addresses reactive service, but it is suitable only for a limited number of organizations, markets, or industries. This is peer-to-peer service and support, though it is better suited to being hosted on the organization's own platform—for example its website—rather than on third–party platforms such as Facebook. This model is that the organization sets up its social media support platform and then invites other customers to respond to—and answer—questions and issues raised by its peers. It operates best where the questions posed have a finite answer; having peers give advice based on limited knowledge is problematic. However, the notion lends itself to the theories of how and why social media works, creating a sense of community among customers. For the organization a compelling reason for using it is that—so long as it is implemented correctly—it is significantly cheaper than other options such as call centers.

## 3.4 Social Hosting

This is the flip side to the Wrangler-George Strait example I give at the beginning of this chapter, where the video was made available on an *owned* platform (wranglernetwork.com), but there have been numerous similar deals where the platform used is a social media platform. Examples include the NBA and *NFL Live* Streams on Facebook, an obvious collaboration between the sports and social media Goliath. As a side note, a cynic might suggest that Facebook Live was developed for this income-generating purpose and not to enhance the general-public user's capability to socially communicate. Facebook, however, is not the only platform to embrace this money-spinning concept, with Twitter's partnership—and that is the correct term—with Seven West Media (SWM), the domestic broadcaster of the Australian Open Tennis being one such example. In 2017 SWM streamed live video and highlights from the Australian Open Tennis Championships. The deal saw SWM deliver video highlights and live footage from the Grand Slam in Melbourne via Twitter. Using the Twitter Amplify platform ("designed to let many more publishers and creators monetize their video content on Twitter, while making it easier for advertisers to reach massive audiences and sponsor great content tweets"[3]) SWM generated income via pre-video advertising for their sponsors. The summer of 2017 saw media and entertainment conglomerate Time Warner Inc. announce a partnership that includes the development of made-for-Snap shows to be delivered exclusively on the company's Snapchat platform. At a more mundane—but more visible— level April 2017 saw LinkedIn introduce *Trending Storylines*—effectively a move to add a *news platform* to its current role as a networking channel.

---

[3] https://blog.twitter.com/2015/twitter-amplify-now-offering-video-monetization-at-scale

# CHAPTER 4

# Strategic Issues in Social Media Marketing

*How can you do anything until you have seen everything, or as much as you can?*

## 4.1 Introduction

Before taking you through this chapter on the subject of *strategic* social media marketing; a confession. I do not think it is possible to have a social media marketing strategy, or even any *digital* marketing strategy. I am, however, going to be a tad pedantic in the use of the words *strategy* and *strategic*—you will note this chapter is *strategic social media marketing*. I believe that the use of the term *strategy* infers some kind of document has been developed by all the parties concerned and that is then developed into a plan that is then disseminated around those interested parties (departments) who then slavishly follow the plan because not to do so "would be more than my job is worth." That might have worked in less volatile world environments in a time when global communication was not really a reality and where the marketers controlled the message that was fed to the buying public who lapped up that message as if it were some kind of benediction. Mr Dylan might have warned us a while ago that "the times they are a changing," but they have not only changed, but continue to change—and in the *digital* environment that change can take place on a daily basis.

So if *strategy* is dead, why long live *strategic*? Well, take any definition you wish of strategy and there will be mention of it being long-term in nature. You will note how the length of that *term* is rarely included within those definitions. It varies from industry to industry, but it is generally accepted to be over a year and probably closer to five years. Let's split the difference and say three years. Three years in *any* digital marketing is the same as a lifetime in the *Mad Men* era of advertising. However, to be successful, any business needs to have some kind of plan that looks forward further than the next Google algorithm change or alteration in Facebook's *Newsfeed*. That plan needs to be fluid enough to be able to react to change or be proactive when opportunities arise, but some aspects of business require longer term planning—*strategic* planning. Finance is the obvious example, something that is generally planned and assessed on an annual basis. Similarly, production requires raw materials to be ordered and shipped long before the production process starts. So there you have it: *strategy* is a formal document; *strategic* is looking beyond day-to-day operations. A bit too simplistic? Yes, but simple generally means easy to understand and implement. Can that be said of any *strategy* you have ever seen?

For those of us that were there, the mid-to-late 1990s was a time when few people (anyone?) *really* understood what the Internet was and how it was going to change both business and the society in which firms traded. From '96 through to '99,[1] I was—among other things—selling websites for a website development company. Apart from spending most of my time explaining to owners and managers—at small- and medium-sized businesses (SMBs) through to national and international brands—what the Internet was (I could do the "... developed for the military ... data in packets ... then came browsers ... yada, yada, yada" speech in my sleep—and probably did) my strongest sales point was that so few organizations had websites that having one gives you a competitive advantage. Of course, that spiel lost its edge as more folk went online, and around that time I found work teaching at a University and so moved away from the sales environment. I had originally only got involved in the whole Internet/e-commerce/e-marketing malarkey as a favor to a couple of friends who were diversifying their book-publishing company—and when I started they had to tell me what the Internet was. However, four

---

[1] At that time the UK was probably a year or so behind the United States in terms of the commercial Internet. Scandinavia was alongside us and we were ahead of the rest of northern Europe by about a year. Southern Europe trailed even further behind, some would suggest it never caught up.

years at the sharp end of the most dynamic industry ever saw me negoti-
ate a very steep learning curve and gave me knowledge and understanding
of the foundations to what we know call *digital marketing*.

It is my opinion—and that of a number of people who were there
at the beginning—that despite the technological advances of the last 20
years the basics of *digital marketing*[2] were established in those early years.
The basics of search engine optimization, for example. However, what I
also brought to the table was a lot of years in retail sales and experience
and qualifications in marketing. I have been saying in classes, conven-
tions, seminars, conferences, bars (well … anywhere) that the Internet
brought nothing *new* to marketing. Better, faster, more efficient ways
of doing things that have been around for years—but nothing new. At
every one of those events I offered a pound (which was worth a lot more
20 years ago than it is now) to anyone who could come up with something that the Internet brought to marketing that did not exist previously.
I have yet to give away a pound. Feel free to join in with my challenge,
but I've got 20 years worth of responses stored up—and remember that
better, faster, more efficient does not mean *new*.

Rant over—back to the book. Well, not really. You see, my potted
history of life in Internet marketing betrays how and why I have the opinions I have about digital marketing in general, and social media marketing in particular. If you like, it represents my qualifications in the subject.
That my experience is *unusual*—but by no means unique—gives me an
insight into the subject that few current practitioners have. I do not hold
myself as some kind of guru, however—I just happened to be in the right
time at the right time with the right experience, and I can write books in
such a way that publishers and the public seem to like. I consider myself
to be a *student* of digital marketing—how can anyone be a master of
something that changes every day? Back in the day I also described myself

---

[2] I currently call it *digital* marketing, but have written books using *online*,
*Internet*, and *e-commerce*. It has also been called *new media*, *cyber*, and a number
of others I don't care to remember. As I say to my students; they are all the same.
Well, not really—e-commerce has come to be the accepted term for making sales
online. Ho hum.

as a one-eyed man in the country of the blind[3]—I knew *something* about marketing on the Internet when most people knew nothing. I still know a bit more than most, but a great many people know more than me about specific elements of digital marketing, including a lot of my ex-students to whom I taught but the basics of the subject.

As I have mentioned previously, there is a serious issue within digital marketing of *experts* in an aspect of the subject (e.g., programmatic advertising) who know nothing of other aspects of digital marketing—let alone marketing in general—because they come from a computer science (i.e., technical) background. We are in a situation where everyone's *an* expert, but no one is *expert*. It is not their fault, but this means they are not in a position to develop anything that is *strategic* in nature. More specifically, the majority of people working in social media do not have marketing backgrounds, be that in experience or education. If you take a look at the title of this chapter, the reason for my personal history should be making a little more sense. That history also gives me an insight into how—in my experience—the growth of commercial websites has a parallel with the growth of commercial social media. It goes back to a time after my "the Internet is coming, it is not a fad" stage when other folk realized there was money to be made in selling websites. The problem was that those folk were almost 100 percent from *technical* and/or *design* backgrounds. They produced websites *they* wanted to produce full of what we called at the time *whistles and bells*. These websites were not developed to meet the needs of the organizations and more importantly their customers, because those developers did not know—or care—about customer needs, satisfying market segments, and so on and so forth. And the business owners and managers were bamboozled by the Internet, networks, HTML, file protocols, servers, and such like. Indeed, truth be known, they were still scared of *computers*. It's also worth mentioning that I sold a lot of websites because I talked to owners and managers about the marketing aspects of a web presence. I left the design and development to our *techies*, but they took their lead from me, often much to their distain. They wanted to include whistle and bells.

---

[3] From the story: "In the land of the blind the one eyed man is king," dating back—probably—to the 16th century.

So when, as part of my work with a university e-commerce research unit, I came across businesses with websites that were performing badly ("It's a chuffin' waste of time this Internet malarkey"), my first question was always: "why do you have a website—what are/were your objectives for it?" Remember, the days of "websites will give you a competitive advantage" had passed, but most answered the question with "because everyone else has got one." I will not bore you further with my response to such comments. I merely gave advice as an *independent* consultant—I worked for a university, I wasn't selling anything. Neither will I go into detail—I assume you know it already—about any website needing to be developed so that it meets its objectives and the needs of its visitors. I'm guessing you are ahead of me at this point—but I am now often asked for my advice on social media marketing ("It's a chuffin' waste of time this social media malarkey"). And so I get out my 20-year old play book and ask: "why have you got a Facebook page—what are/were your objectives for it?" And here's the kicker. As with websites in the 1990s, every one of those owners and/or managers says—like an echo from the past: "we're on Facebook because everyone else is" (note: replace *Facebook* with any social media platform you wish).

And that is why this book has a chapter called *Strategic Social Media Marketing*, and also gives a very big clue into the answers of the titular questions raised in the last two chapters.

Sadly, I must also add that I could have written the above about any aspect of digital marketing by simply doing a *search-and-replace* on the relevant terms. A lack of strategic digital marketing planning—complete with objectives, of course—is commonplace. I would argue that strategic *social* thinking is impossible without a strategic digital plan—and both are impossible without strategic marketing policies. Which, in turn, should be drawn from the overall corporate strategy. If you think I am being a tad left field on this, consider this quote from Marcos de Quintos,[4] who said: "social media is the strategy for those who don't have a true digital strategy." He was prompted to say this as the organization for which he was

---

[4] As part of his presentation at a beverage industry conference in New York and reported on http://adage.com/article/cmo-strategy/coke-cmo-defends-tv-cola-giant-rethinks-digital-approach/307112/

chief marketing officer had pumped significant sums into digital media only to see it outperformed by TV advertising. The company he worked for? They're quite good at this marketing malarkey, you've probably heard of them. Coca-Cola.

Postscript. Just as I come across social media marketing campaigns developed by social media *experts*, I *still* come across too many websites developed by *web design experts* with no marketing skills or experience. But hey-ho, it keeps me busy in consultancy work. And as you now know what your first question should be, you could do the same.

## 4.2 Strategic Objectives

The key strategic objectives for social media marketing can be divided into three parts: (1) core objectives to *any* Internet presence, (2) models that a commercial organization can use in adopting social media for strategic marketing purposes, and (3) key considerations before determining *any* strategic social media marketing objectives. Note that I have presented them in this order, but all need to be addressed before the ultimate decision on objectives can be made. However, if any of the three cannot be agreed or determined then social media marketing should *not* be undertaken—it would be an indication that it would not be the right mode of marketing for the organization, brand, or product. I must also make a disclosure at this point. I have been using these models for a long time, so all of this can be found in some of my other publications, though I have, obviously, made changes to suit the nature of this book. I'm also going to start with a caveat from social media practitioner and author Shama Kabani (2013) who says: "traditional marketing rules cannot be applied to social media because social media is not a marketer's platform. It belongs to consumers." I would agree with her and add that it is something many products, brands, and organizations have failed to appreciate.

### 4.2.1 Core Objectives to Any Internet Presence

Since 1997 I have maintained that in marketing terms, there are three core objectives to any Internet presence or activity (note that my "three objectives" concept was first published in a book I co–authored: Gay et al. (2007) *Online Marketing—a Customer–Led Approach*).

Those three objectives are:

1. Brand development: where the online presence compliments and enhances the offline branding efforts of the organization. However, using social media marketing for this objective is not only effective in building brand awareness, but the capacity for interaction also significantly increases brand affinity. The same caveat that applies to all branding strategies is equally valid in social media marketing brand development. Brand value does not necessarily create a direct increase in sales, but it might increase the company or brand's stock value.

2. Revenue generation: this might also be called *commerce* or *acquisition* and is where the online presence increases revenue into the organization by direct sales, lead generation, or direct marketing—effectively, the message presented should prompt direct action. If any of these objectives is still to be proved effective on—and so relevant to—social media, it is this one. Dubbed by some as *social commerce*, selling things directly from social media has been technically possible for some time, with platforms such as Pinterest actively encouraging businesses to do so (though the cynical among us might suggest that is to boost their own coffers more than any other reason). Research from the Pew Research Center (2016) found that only 15 percent of respondents had "purchased something through a link on a social networking site," my assumption is that this includes adverts—which have a click-thru-rate of less than one percent.[5] In addition, that Twitter mothballed its *Buy button* after only eight months would suggest that social media is hardly worth bothering with for this objective. A caveat to this is that there is a tendency to associate social media marketing with B2C trading, whereas sites that focus on B2B—such as LinkedIn—can be used effectively in lead generation if not direct sales. However, LinkedIn seems to be effective for corporations (IBM, Microsoft, Oracle, GE, for example) and individuals, but not so for SMBs. Also, a quick reminder here: as per my assertion in the previous chapter, advertising on social media is *not* social media marketing.

---

[5] Salesforce Marketing Cloud Advertising Index Q1 2016 Report.

3. Customer care/service/support: where the web is used to enhance the service and support offered to customers. Perhaps to the surprise of many, it is this objective that has proved to be both significant and successful in the social media environment. Eschewing expensive call-center operations and offering customer service and support on the likes of Facebook and Twitter, some organizations have found that an increasing number of people turn first to a social media presence when they experience a problem rather than a website or offline facility.

It is worth noting, however, that having a *primary* object of one of these is that if that objective is achieved then there can be a *spin-off* or *trickle-down* advantage to the other objectives. For example, effective social media customer support can increase the brand's profile.

A footnote to these categories of objective is the issue of *engagement*. It is a constant that practitioners, commentators, and academics speak of engagement when discussion objectives and measurement of social media marketing—indeed, I do so throughout this book. However, there is no definition of what engagement is. I prefer the line of thought whereby any consumer who engages in a conversation with an organization, brand, or product on a social media platform is building a relationship with that organization, brand, or product and so would be in my *branding* category. However, other folk include under engagement such things as clicking on a link to buy a product or asking a product-related question on a social media platform—which come under *income generation* and *support* respectively. Hence, I reject *engagement* as an objective as it is inherent in the three stated categories of objectives.

### 4.2.2 Key Considerations Before Determining Any Strategic Social Media Marketing Objectives

Before embarking on any strategic social media marketing there are six key questions that must be asked… and answered. If the answer to all six is *not* a resounding "yes" then the marketing budget is better spent elsewhere. As Michael Porter famously said: "strategy is about knowing what not to do."

1. Is it *right* for us?

   If the culture of your organization is not *right* for social media marketing then that alone disqualifies it from participation in the discipline. I think this is the absolute key to success or failure in social media marketing—and so have given it a section to itself to round off this chapter. I have made this question number one because if the answer is "no" then asking the other five is a waste of time. However, there is an even wider perspective to this which relates to B2B—it is addressed later in this chapter.

   The organization, brand, or product that questions its suitability for social media marketing could do worse than ask why—other than to make a profit—does the organization exist? Or in marketing terms; what problem is it trying to solve for its customers? The answer to that question goes a long way in determining if social media marketing is *right* for the organization.

2. Is it what our customers expect from us?

   In *pure* marketing terms, if the answer to this question is "yes," then the organization should be active in social media—after all, customers are always right? Aren't they? However, there is a close correlation between this and the previous question in that if the answer to it is "yes" then the answer to this is very likely to be "yes" also because the customers will have already embraced the organization's culture. That said, if customers do expect a social media presence, but the answer to question one is "no," then it is almost certain that the organization's social media efforts will not meet customers' expectations and so the overall result will be a negative experience. Many companies have made ineffective forays into social media for just this misguided *me-too* reason. Sometimes doing nothing is the right thing to do.

3. Is social media worth the effort?

   If we engage in social media marketing will we achieve some kind of return on our investment? This issue is covered in more detail later in this chapter, but essentially any chief financial officer is going to take quite some convincing to sign off on a cost that will never be recovered.

4. Does it fit in with our other marketing efforts?

   Given that this book is about social media marketing, the subject of *offline* strategic marketing is beyond its remit. Nevertheless, it is a frequent failure of *online* marketing initiatives that they are not in sync with the organization's wider strategic efforts. No marketing effort exists in a vacuum and, like all other elements of marketing, to be effective social media marketing *must* be integral to any strategic marketing initiatives.

5. What elements of social media suitable are for our objectives?

   As with other aspects of the organization's marketing (both off- and online) the choice of media and/or platform is established by the objectives of that marketing. This will determine the characteristics of the type of social media on which you need to have a presence, and if there isn't one that is a match, then don't force the issue on an unsuitable platform. Similarly, do not use multiple platforms as a substitute for there not being one that is right. Keeping one social media marketing platform spinning is hard enough, but like the apocryphal plates, if you try to keep too many spinning it is inevitable that they will all eventually crash to the ground.

6. Is it social media marketing?

   This final question is—obviously—a bit different to the previous five, but it is equally valid in it being asked. Essentially, I refer you to the "What social media marketing *is not*" section in the previous chapter. The most obvious *not* is advertising, and hopefully—even if you weren't convinced before—you will appreciate that social media marketing and advertising are two different disciplines that have different strategic objects and those objectives are met by different tactics delivered using different skill sets. I would also suggest that you need to finish the book before you fully appreciate what any social media marketing might hope to achieve.

## 4.3 Return on Investment

Return on investment (ROI), or lack thereof, is the ace I play when arguing that social media marketing is too often practiced by folk who don't understand—or even have knowledge of—marketing. Or knowledge of business. Here's why. Although primarily I teach digital marketing, I am employed as a senior lecturer in marketing, which means I also teach strategic marketing. I drum home to my students that any marketing tactic, campaign, or strategy must bring in more money than it costs. Marketers will appreciate that this is problematic where branding is concerned, but ultimately the same rule applies. I would argue that if an advert is placed in a local newspaper, it must increase sales by enough to realize an increased profit (that is, sales less fixed and variable costs). If it doesn't then you should not place the advert (again, branding issues aside). Hardly rocket science, is it? Yet so many owners and managers get it wrong. In the previous chapter I made the point that social media marketing is not free. I repeat. Social. Media. Marketing. Is. Not. Free. Got it? I'm assuming that you appreciate; (a) how important this is, and (b) how relevant I think this is to any social media marketing strategy. And yet I see reference to the allusion that social media marketing is free on an almost daily basis—frequently stated or written by folk who should know better. Or should they? Maybe they are not marketers? Or perhaps they are perpetrators of the legend of the Emperor's New *Digital* Clothes?

A brief example from my own experience is a university (not the one at which I work) recruitment team that was encouraged by management to use social media as a significant part of its marketing efforts. Two new members of staff were recruited to work the social media desk. Each was paid £25K per annum. A rough calculation for a UK university in determining the cost of an employee is to multiply their wage by 2.5, so these new additions to the payroll would cost the organization around £125K a year. I asked the recruitment manager what the return on that investment would be. He had no idea. Nor did he have any idea how to calculate it—or any real evidence that social media marketing actually had a role to play in students' decision-making process. I then asked if, in a time of constantly reducing budgets, he could use the £125K in a more *traditional* way that had clear measurement for ROI—recruitment fairs was my suggestion. Oh yes, he replied without hesitation. I imparted the fable of the dodgy tailors who made an imaginary set of clothes for the Emperor. His shoulders slumped. As we were in the bar after a recruitment event I bought him a drink. It seemed the least I could do.

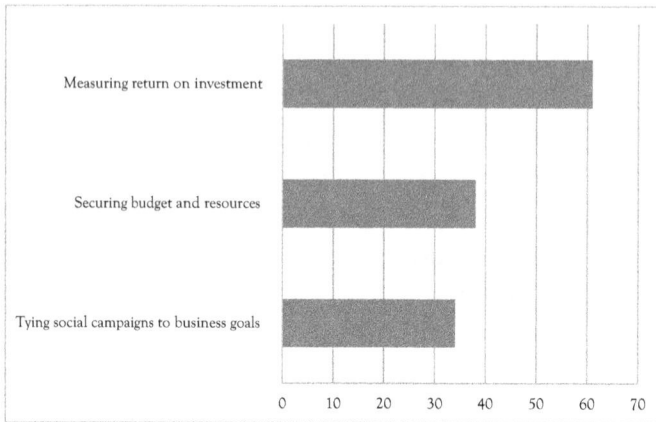

*Figure 4.1 The top challenges for social media marketers*

University marketers are not the only ones to have questions about any ROI from spending on social media marketing.

The 2016 SimplyMeasured *State of Social Marketing Annual Report* revealed that measuring ROI was the top challenge identified by 61 percent of marketers—with securing resources (38 percent) and tying social to business goals (34 percent) the next two. The same organization's 2017 Report found that few marketers are using revenue and conversion metrics as their standards (see Figure 4.1).

Similarly, *the Highlights & Insights* of the CMO Survey[6] for *February 2017 found that* only 37 percent of marketers say they can produce quantitative proof of the impact of social media spend. This could mean they are not using the correct methods of measurement—but I read it as more evidence that social media marketing is not giving a significant ROI. At least these statistics might be interpreted as an improvement on findings from the same organization's February 2016 CMO Survey. It found that only 3.4 percent of marketing leaders reported that social media contributes *very highly* to the organization's performance, with 40 percent reporting a below average contribution. The CMO Surveys make no

---

[6] Ongoing research funded by a partnership between Deloitte LLP, Duke University's Fuqua School of Business, and The American Marketing Association. See cmosurvey.org.

mention of how much the respondents had spent on those disappointing social media marketing efforts—but if they are looking for some kind of *return*, there must have been *investment*. I would like to see an additional question added to these otherwise excellent surveys, it would be something like: "Do you, or have you ever, made similar levels of investment in any other aspect of marketing that consistently gives such a poor return on that investment?" I have asked that question many times of many people. The answer normally gives me the opening to relate a story about two crooked tailors. Compare this with the *OnBrand Magazine's State of Branding Report 2017*,[7] which found that 65 percent of marketing executives and brand managers surveyed had no plans to invest in new technologies such as 360-degree video, virtual reality (VR), augmented reality (AR), chatbots, and beacons in 2017. Proof of ROI was cited as the key issue. So why have so many marketers taken on social media marketing whilst at the same time questioning its ability to return any investment. My only conclusion is that they think that—unlike virtual and augmented reality—it is both free and easy to implement.

If the reason behind questionable ROI is related to the methods of measurement—or lack thereof—there are some who would suggest that using the *correct* methods only serve to prove the failings of social media marketing. Research from Sign-Up Technologies (2013) is representative of similar surveys—and I can find no recent research to suggest it is not still valid—suggesting that the average click-through-rate (CTR) for a tweet is 1.64 percent. That is: when a marketing tweet is sent with a link to a further marketing message, less than two in a hundred will click on that link. The CTR for direct marketing e-mails is accepted as being around 3 percent. However, it is relatively easy to send tens of thousands of e-mails to targeted lists—tweets are not so targeted. Obviously, some organizations, brands, and products have thousands of followers, but Sign-Up's research also found that the CTR dropped to less than 0.5 percent for accounts with over 10K followers. That's 50 people in 10 thousand—50 people who may or may not have an interest in whatever the marketing message might be. Switched-on businesses will know what

---

[7] https://blog.bynder.com/en/state-of-branding

percentage of these 50 people will make a purchase—or whatever the objective of the campaign is—and so it would be easy to work out the return on investment. The first section of the next chapter will help assess just what that investment might be, but these figures suggest that the return isn't going to be anything to write home about. Sign-Up Technologies' research asked no questions with reference to the costs involved in producing the ineffective social media marketing campaigns with such poor CTRs.

In the next chapter operational issues related to the implementation of a social media marketing strategy are covered—and every one of those issues costs money. At the *very least*, there is the time it takes to write each tweet or Facebook entry. And the cheapest scenario is to have an existing employee do that, which moves the cost into an existing fixed cost. Except that whilst they are writing the tweet those staff are not doing the job they were employed to do before they were given the social media writing task. Throw in the fact that such an ad hoc method of engaging in social media marketing is unlikely to be effective—it may even be damaging to the brand—and you have a negative ROI. If there is no profit, don't do it.

Furthermore, there is the question of *why* people follow the organization, brand, or product on social media. As previously stated, it is my contention that the majority follow because they are already a satisfied customer. Yes, I know the concept of relationship marketing, and I know it costs more to find a new customer than retain an existing one—but isn't it a reasonable assumption that a customer who *follows* would continue to purchase products whether they are on social media or not or whether they have *liked* the organization or not? The key issue, therefore, becomes; is gathering followers going to increase takings at the checkout? I suspect it is not.

My final comment in this section is to make it clear that ROI for social media marketing has been a question I have been raising for some time. In 2010 in an online musing I asked the question: "What's the ROI in using twitter?" and attempted to put some numbers to the cost of Dell's social media efforts which, as I said at the time, was "often held as a poster-child for the use of Twitter as a marketing tool." A year later I turned my attention to Facebook. Interestingly—at least to me—is that I include the comment that; "it would seem that the Facebook evangelist bandwagon is threatening to steamroller all in front of it." It is, in my opinion, the evangelist bandwagon that is responsible for peddling the Emperor's New *Digital* Clothes.[8]

## 4.4 Measure and Monitor

If there is a constant in the results of research into social media marketing, particularly at a strategic level, it is that respondents find it difficult to measure any return on investment—or lack thereof. Having determined that social media marketing is an option for the organization, brand, or product, and then identifying suitable objectives and the platforms on which they might be achieved; then comes the issue of how to monitor that marketing so that an assessment of ROI can be made. Marketers who were early exponents of social media marketing followed conventional wisdom and assumed that audience size was the most important measure of success. They did little more than set up a social presence and worked hard to gain *fans, followers, friends*, or *likes* by a series of tactics that owed more to traditional marketing than the new social medium. Contests and *like-bait* content might have succeeded in running up a *follower* count— but they did nothing to encourage connection and relevance.

Furthermore, it is easy for such simple metrics to mask the truth. One investigation that perhaps I inspired—but did not actively participate in—involved a vegetarian sandwich stall on a chic market in a fashionable part of London. However, these were no ordinary sandwiches. Produced individually with enthusiasm and passion by two sisters, they were individual works of art, and—as they say—*to die for*. An ex-student of mine worked nearby, and being a vegetarian was soon a regular customer. The popularity of the sandwiches grew, and with it, the business. So much so that it won a local award and the sisters became local business celebrities. When asked in an interview for a magazine about their marketing the sisters said it was 100 percent down to Instagram, onto which they posted pictures of their culinary creations. Followers on the image-based platform

[8] These stories are available on: alancharlesworth.eu/alans-musings/whats-the-ROI-on-tweeting.html and alancharlesworth.eu/alans-musings/whats-the-ROI-in-using-facebook.html.

peaked at nearly 30,000. However, I had taught my ex-student well, and she was as skeptical as me. So—with the permission of the sisters—she did a bit of research. It turns out that the vegetarian side of things had been championed by like-minded social media folk, with a great deal of *me-too* followers all around the world. Yes, that is *all around the world*, as in: realistically, never going to be customers. So my ex-student did some old-fashioned leg-work research, and stood next to the stall and asked questions. Wisely, the questions did not focus on social media. The results were that many regular customers followed the sisters on Instagram, but only *after* becoming regulars. The multiple images sent daily were routinely ignored by the majority—though some did select their sandwich for the day from a message sent that morning. None thought they bought more sandwiches because of the Instagram messages. Many customers had used social media to tell friends about the stall, but on their personal pages (i.e., *social* not *marketing*). And the main reason for repeat custom? The *right* product, in the *right* place, at the *right* time, at the *right* price. And how did most customers become aware of the stall? Mostly: word-of-mouth, shopping at the market, or the publicity generated by the business award. On the plus side, the Instagram activity—a quick photo on a smartphone and post on their site—took up very little of the sisters' time and cost nothing. If *posing* each sandwich, taking the pic, and posting it took only 30 seconds—and the sisters did that (on average) 15 times a day—that is seven and a half minutes a day of not making sandwiches and not serving customers. Multiply the numbers up over a year and that's around a week of sandwich making/selling time lost. 30,000 followers sounds great, but the impact of social media marketing on their sales would seem to be minimal. I refer you to the previous section of this chapter.

Although he did not realize he was predicting a problem that is now commonplace with regard to the wider use of the amount of data available to businesses and marketers, when asked—in 2011—about his organization's stance toward social media measurement, Irfan Kamal, senior vice president, digital/social strategy at Ogilvy & Mather said:

> We need to measure metrics that are related to business value. Does social media change brand perception? Does it increase consideration? Does it drive actual sales for the brand? What

often gets measured instead are … diagnostic or optimization metrics—the number of Facebook fans, the Twitter follower base, the size of a group or a message board or a LinkedIn group. All the metrics that are easily visible are the ones that end up getting measured most often. The problem is that it's unclear whether there is a direct relationship between these metrics and genuine business value.

Wise words that certainly described the general state of *social* affairs at that time. Sadly, some years later, it is still too often the way many organizations treat social media marketing metrics. That said, identifying what to measure in assessing the effectiveness of social media marketing can be problematic. Therefore, building desired outcomes into strategic planning is a logical step—and one that is a viable solution compared to common practice that has organizations (1) performing some social media marketing, (2) collecting some data, and then (3) trying to reconcile the two. Given the perennial issue of managers using data to justify expenditure—and so, their jobs—the results of such spurious analysis are skewed results based on data that has been *interpreted* to suit the manager's needs. Completing no analysis is better than this practice as at least there would be no time and resources wasted in the exercise.

McDonald et al (2014) propose that social media metrics can be classified into one of four broad categories:

1. The type and sentiment of the content—for example, text, image, video, and positive or negative.
2. Delivery—the number of times the content has been seen by users.
3. User responses to the content—likes, shares, comments, downloads, for example.
4. Properties of the users in contact with the content—such as physical location, preferences.

These could be used as metrics from which hypotheses and models could be developed. At a practical level, the following is a list of things that might be considered for measuring. Note that I have used as a foundation a list developed by Heidi Cohen for her excellent analysis of the extremely successful 2010 Old Spice social media campaign. It goes without saying that while some of the following are straight counts—particularly the financial aspects—others may need some data collection prior to the campaign for post-event comparison. It is also the case that the analytics of some may need to be sourced offline. The issues are divided into two categories: branding and finance.

**Brand indicators** (note how Ms Cohen categorizes *engagement* as an aspect of branding—as do I in Chapter 4 (Section 4.2) where I discuss strategic objectives of social media marketing).

- Engagement (i). Did the campaign increase likes and followers? Were posts forwarded or re-tweeted? Did existing social media followers increase their activity?
- Engagement (ii). Did the campaign increase engagement on the organization's own website(s) via click-through from social media?
- Share of voice. How mentions of your brand on the social media pages of others, plus forwarded and re-tweeted posts, compare to those of your competitors?
- Target market. Did the campaign increase awareness in key target markets?
- Brand sentiment. Did brand perceptions change? Was this in line with campaign goals?
- Purchase intent. Did the campaign result in increased buyer likelihood to purchase?
- Loyal fans. Did the campaign reinforce a positive perception of users who feel an affiliation and affection for the brand?
- Brand status. Did the campaign increase brand recognition?
- Line extensions. Did the campaign's branding impact extend to other of the organization's products?
- Market share. Did the product and/or brand's market share increase?
- Competition. Did the campaign have an impact on direct competitors' sales?

**Financial indicators** (note that this involves a retrospective examination of actual costs that can then be compared to those predicted before the event).

- Revenue (i). What were sales for the promoted product?
- Revenue (ii). What sales were generated via click-through from social media platforms?
- Marketing expenses. How much did the social media campaign cost including all related expenses?
- Other expenses. Did the campaign have other costs due to incremental technology and server capacity needs?
- Headcount. Were additional personnel, direct staff, and/or consultants required to handle the campaign and its complexity?
- Profitability. How did this campaign impact the product and brand's profitability?
- Investor relations. Did this campaign have any impact on perceptions of the company as a whole, its stock price, and/or investor perception?

Good news for the social media marketer is that since that Old Spice campaign, tools for social media data gathering and analysis have been developed by numerous software vendors. Much of this software can be made bespoke to the organization's requirements, but some of the more basic measurement tools include the following:

- Website analytics tools to track the actions of visitors who arrive on the website via social media platforms or initiatives.
- Social media monitoring tools that monitor the various platforms for posts, tweets, or conversations that are relevant to the product, brand, or organization.
- Social site-specific tools, commonly provided by the platform's publishers with more complex versions from specialist vendors.

- Influencer identification tools that are used to identify those social influencers that the product, brand, or organization might wish to engage with.

The capability of these products has expanded significantly due to a combination of social media adoption, client needs, and advances in technology.

The availability of monitoring software brings us to another potential objective for what might be described as an element of social media marketing—that of using social media purely as a source of information as part of the organization's market intelligence gathering efforts. In essence: listen to what is being said on social media but don't get involved in it (hence the practice being known as *social listening*). Before going any further it is worth reminding readers that all the traits of good practice for research apply equally to social media research. The collection of pertinent data has always been determined by the three Vs: volume, velocity, and variety. It is too often the case that digital technology enables the relatively easy collection of high volumes of data—some would argue the rise of so-called *Big Data* is a result of this.

Before employing software—be it off-the-shelf or bespoke—to collect copious amounts of data, marketers need to be sure that: (a) they possess the skills and time to analyze that data, and (b) data can be translated into *information* that is to the organization—that is, it can be used to either improve the organization's performance or identify failings of it. If these two issues cannot be confirmed, then collection of data is a waste of time and resources. Harping back to the title of this chapter, such research should be conducted at a strategic level with adequate resources and any resulting information being processed and fed into the marketing decision-making process. This differs from, for example, the way in which Twitter might be monitored by the social service team so that customer enquiries can be responded to or the public relations team might look for issues that fall under their remit. However, as is the case with the gathering of any strategic market intelligence, all staff that has a role in the organization's social media at an operational level should be encouraged to share with the market intelligence department any data, information, or events that they feel can be used at a more strategic level.

Monitoring of user activity on pertinent social media platforms is usually made easier by the platforms themselves providing analytics data, often at no charge. This can provide valuable information. Increased visits to a Pinterest image of a particular brand of product or increased mention of that product on Twitter might prompt a retailer to promote that product on their website or retail outlet, for example. Similarly, planners of an event—a music festival, perhaps—could monitor social media conversations to help estimate interest and potential attendance, or concerns that may be putting people off attending; a perceived shortage of camping or toilet facilities, possibly. Such issues could then be addressed by the marketers. A further use of *social listening* is to help judge public feeling about a happening or incident involving or relevant to, the organization, brand, or product. An example of this is the United Airlines' PR disaster when staff forcibly removed an *overbooked* passenger from one of the company's flights. Rather than playing down the incident, if United's PR and/or social team had monitored social media immediately after the event unfolded they would have seen just how big a social media furore was taking place globally. Similarly, in the run up to the U.S. Presidential election in November 2016, social media monitors noted from social conversations and postings that Donald Trump was far more popular than Hilary Clinton than the opinion polls were suggesting.

There is, however, another form of research into social media user activity. This is based on the offline concept of *ethnography*: "overt or covert participation in the everyday lives of people over an extended period of time" (Hammersley and Atkinson 1995) and was dubbed *netnography* (Internet-ethnography) in an early study by Kozinets (1997). This online version of a social science involves the researchers joining social media sites and entering into community discussion.

However, this kind of research is questioned on ethical grounds by some social scientists. To garner useful data the researchers must actively engage in the social media conversation rather than simply observing and monitoring what others are doing and saying. This raises the moral question of whether or not the researchers should disclose their (true) identity and purpose. The key issue is that (a) if the researchers act as another person their contribution could sway any conversation, and (b) if the researchers' *true* identity is revealed the users may change their behavior—if they accept the researcher into the group at all.

It is often the case, however, that such complex research methods overlook valuable data that is sitting on social media sites just waiting to be harvested. It may be time consuming—though software is available—but by trawling social media sites such as LinkedIn, researchers might identify potential customers, competitors, or just the movers and shakers within a market or industry. What other people in the industry have to say about their own and the researchers' organizations, brands, and products might also prove useful.

Although I would consider it to belong in a book on market research rather than one on social media marketing, there is also the use of social platforms as a channel to disseminate and collect market research. This could be anything from simple click one-answer questions, through hosting questionnaires to forum-type focus groups.

## 4.5 Legal Issues Impacting on Social Media Marketing

I have no intention, or the necessary expertise, to start addressing the legal issues that impact on social media marketing. My general advice at this point is to say: "pay someone who is qualified to advise you." That said, there are a couple of issues that are worthy of attention. The first is that the legal department has a role to play in the day-to-day operations in that they must be prepared to be indulgent with regard to allowing negative comments, and even abuse, to remain on the organizations social media presence and give marketers the opportunity to respond in the social media philosophy rather than resorting to the letter of the law. Secondly, and there is more of this issue in the next chapter with regard to its impact on marketing, any member of staff who writes something on any social media platform that is *owned* by the organization is a legal representative of that organization. Nuff said?

Other legal issues to note include:

- Paying influencers is advertising—says the Federal Trade
  Commission (FTC)—and all ads must be identified as such.
  If an organization as big as Warner Bros can fall foul of
  this—as they did in late 2014—so might anyone. The UK's
  Ad Watchdog called out Oreo around the same time for not

having *vloggers* on YouTube make it clear they were being paid to endorse the biscuits (that's *cookies* in their homeland). Of course, having a real person start their *vlog* entry with: "the makers paid me to say this" pretty much defeats the objective of the social media marketing exercise.

- In March 2016, the German courts ruled that German websites with Facebook *Like* buttons (i.e., "Like us on Facebook") must include cookie-like disclosures with regard to the company transferring data to or from Facebook (I wonder how many users realize that happens? Or care?). Note to U.S. readers; in the EU, where Germany goes others generally follow.

- Pretty much as I write this in December 2016, the Consumer Review Fairness Act has passed through legislation. This should not concern *genuine* marketers however—the Act is designed to stop unscrupulous businesses adding "non-disparagement" clauses to their terms and conditions of consumer reviews of service agreements, that is, "if you say bad things we'll sue you."

- Back to the EU, not only is overt commenting on review sites (e.g., going on TripAdvisor and saying *your own* hotel is the best in town) a questionable practice in marketing terms, but in Europe under Part 2 of The Consumer Protection from Unfair Trading Regulations 2008 (which addresses issues of misleading actions) it is likely to be deemed an offence.

You have been warned.

## 4.6 Culture

Within academia—practitioners don't *really* care—there is a constant debate over whether marketing is an art or a science. In recent years the *science* argument has gained strength on the back of digital applications—computers, programs, and algorithms are all science aren't they? My feet, however, are firmly planted in the art camp. Science can help marketers make decisions, but science cannot make those decisions. Though much trumpeted, current applications of artificial intelligence (AI) do little more than decide which is the best option based on what has been included on its database. Scientific study is frequently based on the assumption that there is a specific answer to every question, generally known as *positivism*. This is fine if all the variables or units remain the same. For example, if you add together the same amount of substance "a" to substance "c" in a controlled environment at a set temperature there will be a fixed result. That result is the same now as when it was first conducted—and will be in the future. And it will be same result if the experiment is conducted in Chicago, Beijing, or London.

In marketing, however, we can't even agree on what our variables and units are (add *some* advertising to some *sales*?) let alone find a controlled environment. The environment in which marketing is practiced—and researched—is made up of human beings. Humans are pesky critters who have a tendency to be different. They have differing thoughts and opinions based on individual experiences. And they are different if they are from Chicago, Beijing, or London. Marketing research—I believe—can at best be *interpretivist*, where any theory applies only in the time, place, and environment in which the *experiment* takes place. Marketing cannot have any laws or bodies of theory that are, as in science, universal. Ergo, marketing is not a science. An example of my somewhat naive view on scientific research comes from an organization who are one of the world's leaders in re-marketing (if you put an item in an online shopping basket but do not complete the purchase the seller contacts you to encourage you to complete the purchase). They were conducting *scientific* research into the timeliness of the "you can still buy it" message, and so did multivariate testing sending the same message at timed intervals. After several hundred thousand messages had been sent and responses recorded it was decided—scientifically—that $x$ minutes (I seem to recall it was around 37) was the optimum period for sending the message. However, the whole exercise was conducted by computer scientists. And very clever they are in their field, but I find that computer scientists are poor swimmers in the murky waters of marketing because, basically, they are not marketers. I am, and I asked if they changed the message as the time-to-contact increased? Or if the message was different for different products? Or if the time of the day (in whatever time zone the customer was in) was factored into the optimum time delay? Or if the customers were male or female? Or what age group they belonged to? Or if the canceled purchase was made on a PC or mobile device? Hopefully, you've caught my drift here—the environment in which the experiment was conducted was different for every single one of those customers and their decision to complete the sale (or not) was made in their own head at a time of their choosing. That the optimal time for a response was $x$ minutes was pure chance.

So why this wander into the prickly terrain of science versus art? Well, that's because I do not think you can measure the titular subject of this section. And why is that so important? It is important because *culture* is the key to social media marketing success or failure. Without it being *right* social media marketing will not work, no matter how well its elements are addressed. With it being *right*, you can overcome deficiencies in other areas. And it is the whole issue of what is the *right* culture for social media marketing that cannot be identified scientifically. *Right* is a gut feeling. You cannot measure or meter it. You cannot assess or examine it. You cannot reproduce it or fake it. You cannot convert to it. It is the way the organization, brand, or product *is*. The way it works. The way it operates. It is a management style—or *style* of management. Taylor's *Scientific Management* won't cut it in social media and neither will any organization that is unwilling to empower its employees or encourage them to take risks without a committee having discussed it first. Indeed, an organization that makes decisions via committees isn't *right* for social media. It's the way it treats its staff. It is its staff. It is what staff do if the manager doesn't tell them what to do. It is its leader. It is informal rather than formal. It is what it is. If the organization has to ask if it is *right*, it isn't. It is just *right* for social media marketing or it is not.

The nature of the product—and remember that in marketing terms the product can be tangible or intangible (a service)—will also play a part. Some products lend themselves to social media marketing. Some don't. Some brands lend themselves to social media marketing. Some don't. Some generate passion in their buyers, some don't. A caveat is that a product and/or brand might be suitable, but if the organizational culture isn't *right* then social media marketing won't work. Conversely, an organization with the right culture can take a product and/or brand that is not considered suitable for social media marketing and make it work. Such is the nature of the *right* organization. To be effective in the social media environment there must be an almost automatic—organic, if you will—affinity to the way the product, brand, or organization acts in that environment. In other words, it already acts that way in the real world, so social media is a natural step to take. Whether we call it the *culture*, the *ethos* of the *philosophy* of the product, brand, or organization, it is its very nature that defines the way it trades and the relationship it has with its customers.

If culture is hard to identify as being *right* for social media marketing, identifying products that might be suitable is easier—but remember, the organizational culture still has to be *right*. There are a whole bunch of *possibles*: anything related to the entertainment industry; ditto sports; anything that is online only; anything that has some kind of personality (if it does, that suggests the organization is right, as the organization will have created that personality); anything that is in a niche market; anything related to a hobby; anything people talk about at the water cooler or down at the pub. Of course exceptions exist, and my problem in this argument is that they tend to be the ones that get the most publicity—and so we have the Emperor's New *Digital* Clothes—"if it works for something so boring, it must work for us." What I've just given you—you would have thought—is the foundation of a list as long as your arm of products suitable for social media marketing. But whoa there, rein back that excitement. The list of *not suitables* is almost infinite.

As a general rule—again, with notable exceptions—B2B trading does not lend itself to social media marketing. B2B tends to be formal, it is *business* after all, but B2C *can* be fun. Commentators suggest that humor is essential if social media marketing is to be successful. Guess what? Some organizations, brands, or products are just not funny. Furthermore, although the product might lend itself to humor, the organizational culture might not suit *funny*. B2B represents the vast majority of trading, realistically only shops or retail services deal with the end user, every other business sells its product or service to another business. And yes, before you say as much, I appreciate some firms sell to another business but their marketing efforts are aimed at the end consumer, fast moving consumer goods (FMCG) and cars being obvious examples, and many of those offer potential for social media marketing. My point about B2B products is that they are not marketed in the same way as B2C products. To test my assertion, take a look around you wherever you are as you read this—be that office, classroom, library, train, bus, airport… wherever. Now identify and list things that have been sold by someone to someone else. Some will be B2C; yours or other people's clothes, for example. If you are at home, some of what you can see will have been sold (to you) in a retail environment. If you are in any kind of commercial space, what you see will have been sold to the owners of that space in a B2B transaction. OK so far? I'm guessing your list (mental or otherwise) is made up of *complete* products?

In my case, I'm in my home office and so as you can imagine, my list would be: table, PC, keyboard, mouse, mousemat, speakers, reading lamp, post-it notes, pens, and so on and so forth. But that's my B2C stuff. What about the light switch, power sockets, window frame, door, door handles, door hinges, light fittings, and radiator that were bought by the house builder from a variety of suppliers. Then there's the packaging in which all those goods were transported, stored, and sold. Furthermore, there are the component parts of everything on your list. The manufacturer of my extendible reading lamp, for example, will not have made the springs used on it; they will have been bought from whoever makes—and markets—springs. The same goes for the wire, switch, and bulb—and the metal and plastic that is formed into the shape of a lamp stand and its shade. Much of my consultancy and research is for and with this kind of business—particularly small to medium size businesses—and the way in which trade exists in those industries along with the expectations of customers, plus the nature of the products (most are pretty boring) all adds up to social media marketing not being suitable for those organizations. Going back to your list of products seen from where you are. Do you appreciate what I mean about the list of goods *not* suitable for social media marketing being *almost* infinite? Note that for many years I have conducted this *look at the products around you* exercise in strategic marketing classes. The objective is to make marketing students aware that marketing is not all Apple, Nike, and BMW, and in particular that B2B is very different to B2C.

An—if not *the*—exception to the *culture must be right* rule is LinkedIn. This is mainly because it is B2B in nature and design, but also because the writers tend to be individuals, even if they are representing organizations,

brands, or products. It is also because LinkedIn users are there for a purpose which is almost formal, whereas other social media platforms favor
the informal. LinkedIn is about work, not pleasure.

In the B2B environment there is often a relationship between the
buyer and seller that exists offline and in private, not played out in public
on a social media site. Certainly if I were a buyer for Wal-Mart, I would
expect sellers—with whom I might be spending millions of dollars each
week—to show me a little more respect than communicating with me
via Facebook or a tweet. The State of Pipeline Marketing report (Pipeline
Marketing 2016), which focuses on how B2B marketers drive growth,
includes data not only on the channels used by B2B marketers, but how
effective they feel those channels are. This data is shown in Table 4.1.
I should add that these findings pretty much match my own experiences,

**Table 4.1  The most popular and effective B2B marketing channels**

|  | Marketing activities/ channels used to acquire customers (%) | Activity/channel that makes the most positive impact on revenue (%) |
| --- | --- | --- |
| E-mail marketing | 88.6 | 8.3 |
| Social media | 85.0 | 3.1 |
| Content marketing | 81.2 | 9.1 |
| Search engine optimization | 78.0 | 9.1 |
| Word-of-mouth/referrals | 74.9 | 22.0 |
| Conference/trade shows | 74.5 | 9.1 |
| Search advertising | 59.6 | 6.7 |
| Public relations | 59.2 | 1.2 |
| Outbound calling | 58.0 | 8.3 |
| Retargeting | 52.5 | 0.8 |
| Partner marketing | 48.6 | 5.1 |
| Display advertising | 47.5 | 0.8 |
| Video advertising | 22.0 | 0.8 |
| TV, radio, and print ads | 12.5 | 0.4 |
| Other | 2.5 | 4.3 |

with the exception that the elements that involve personal contact are commonly used more and so generate most income.

In general, the chart shows clearly just how different B2B marketing is to B2C. Specific to this book, however, is that so many indulge in social media marketing and yet recognize its shortcomings. A witness for the prosecution in the case of the Emperor's New *Digital* Clothes perhaps? A final observation, prompted by my own research and experience, but reinforced by the State of Pipeline Marketing Report finding is that just because an organization, brand, or product has a presence on social media does not mean it is practicing *effective* social media marketing.

# CHAPTER 5

# Operational Issues in Social Media Marketing

*Gardens are not made by singing "Oh, how beautiful!" and sitting in the shade*

## 5.1 Management and Staff

As is always the case when considering strategic and operational issues, there is a convergence between the two—and social media marketing is no exception. The first topic, that of who *owns* the organization's social media marketing endeavors, is one that could be considered strategic or operational. By *owns*, I mean who calls the shots, takes the plaudits when it works and brickbats when it doesn't? For *ownership* you could read *responsibility*. Any organization-wide initiative—for social media marketing needs to be that—is impossible to control and manage without a single point of *ownership*. As you might expect from a marketer, I say that *social* comes under the remit of the marketing department, possibly those responsible for any strategic integrated marketing communications the organization might have. However, if strategic responsibility lies within the marketing department, it is not necessarily the case that marketing is where *operational* control necessarily belongs. To be most effective, social media marketing is best delivered by staff that have the ability to write effectively and with the necessary skills, training, and education to represent the product, brand, or organization in the social media environment. Although some marketers may possess these abilities, it is more likely that the necessary skills be found in the public relations (PR) department as it is commonly the case that PR staff have either journalistic backgrounds or have studied journalistic skills as part of a public relations-based education program. However, too frequently PR staff lack the relevant education and/or experience to see the role *social* plays in the organization's wider strategic marketing. If management expect a small marketing staff to add social to their workload and be effective at it, then the organization is not *right*. If they recognize its potential value and importance (they *get* it), management will commit to providing the necessary resources. It is also the case that the person appointed to manage social media marketing (whatever his or her title) must also act as a champion for the cause. Which, in turn, means they must be a natural part of that culture, ethos, or whatever it is that makes the organization *right* for social media marketing. Essentially, they have to *get* social media. The closest comparison I can offer is that of the managing editor of a newspaper: the output of the two jobs is similar, but successful editors *get* the publishing business. And that, in turn, is problematic as social media is generally best understood by the younger generation who would not normally be considered for relatively senior management roles.

If identifying the manager for social media marketing is problematic, the same issue is repeated for staff. They must have the prerequisite writing skills, but they must also possess *soft skills* such as multitasking capabilities, patience, flexibility, dedication, and a good sense of humor. Indeed, it is an argument that as in many customer service jobs, staff should be recruited on their soft skills as they cannot be taught in the same way that hard skills can. Furthermore, folk with the requisite hard skills are not suitable for social media roles if their personalities do not match the job's soft-skill requirements. Suitable staff are also very likely to part of Generation Y—the Millennials—which in itself can be problematic. By definition, these folks are relatively young, and so may not have the maturity and common sense that comes with age and experience.

Essentially, anyone who sees working on social media marketing as a *job* is not right for the job. But if the organization has the *right* culture, its staff would not have a work ethic of *it's just a 9-to-5 job*. I'll go further: if the organizational culture is *right* for social media marketing, the staff to work in it are probably already employed by the organization and would be fighting to be involved—it would be in their nature. Purveyors of the Emperor's New *Digital* Clothes are quick to champion the successes of organizations that have these traits—but it is my experience that such organizations are few and far between, and vastly outnumbered by those that do not possess those characteristics. We simply do not hear of attempts at social media marketing that are dead in the water. Trawl though Facebook to see where the bodies lie.

A key issue for managers is one that is often the option of choice for organizations when faced with introducing new operations—that of outsourcing. As with all aspects of marketing, there are agencies who will take on the social media marketing for the product, brand, or organization. While this is an effective alternative to creating a new department and recruiting or reallocating staff, outsourced operations will still require someone—or department—to oversee those operations and co-ordinate them within the organization. Although outsourcing was a popular route in the early days of social media marketing, many organizations found there was a lack of control over social media output in their name and many have reverted to inhouse operations. That said, it would be my observation that if social was outsourced that in itself would tend to suggest that the organization, brand, or product was not *right* for social media marketing in the first place.

The final item for this section is one that pervades all digital marketing. It is also something that is beginning to be raised by those in some position of authority or repute who appreciate the problem. It is also something I have railed against since I got involved in this whole *digital* malarkey in 1996—so if this section comes across as a bit of a rant; it is.

My point of contention is this: Digital marketing is *marketing*. Ergo social media marketing is *marketing*. Any social media marketing will take place with a wider digital marketing strategy. Any digital marketing will take place as just one aspect of any strategic marketing initiatives undertaken by the organization. However, too often I come across digital *marketers* who do not know even the fundamentals of marketing. These folk may well be good—excellent even—at one aspect of digital marketing (search engine optimization is an obvious example), but they do not appreciate how that element is—or should be—an integral part of a wider digital operation. Which means they certainly do not understand how *their* relatively small element fits into the organization's strategic marketing. And it gets worse. These folk are being promoted to positions of *digital managers*, or even—the author puts palms to side of head in The Scream-esque fashion—*marketing managers*. That's a recipe for a disaster waiting to happen. Similarly, these folks are finding jobs writing about digital marketing. Not necessarily books, I hasten to add, but—and this impacts on the *definitions* issue raised elsewhere in the book—online blogs, newsletters, and websites. And not just blogs read only by one man and his dog. In one top industry online publication I read an article that said: "Return on Investment (ROI) has rapidly become a buzzword among marketers: a phrase that is often used, but rarely defined." Author adopts *Scream* pose again. Sadly, the young writer is correct in that these *non-marketing marketers* have never come across the concept. However, for anyone who has studied marketing, ROI is a prerequisite of any marketing strategy, tactic, or campaign. It is business 101—and marketing is part of business. And as for "rarely defined," what's simpler than *returns should exceed costs?*

Furthermore, it is my experience that these non-marketing digital marketers come from technical and/or computer science backgrounds where their degree and/or experience does not include *any* knowledge and understanding of strategic marketing—of which digital is just one part. A quick glance at any strategic marketing textbook of a degree program syllabus will suggest that not only is *digital* about a tenth of all marketing, but that it comes near the end where it requires the reader/learner to understand the basics before studying that element.

This scenario is also widespread in academia. It seems that many—even the majority—of academic articles that I read on digital marketing are not written by folk with marketing qualifications. Presumably that is because marketing is so easy anyone can do it? Note: if it was so easy why would even a single business or product fail?

Because it is pertinent to my argument, I'm going to throw in a reminder of my background here. I am not anti-digital, nor am I a *digital* marketing luddite (yes, I appreciate they do exist). This is my ninth book on the subject. For many years I was an Internet evangelist ("it's not a fad, it's not going away, it's going to change the way we do business"), neither am I anti computer scientist. I openly admit that if you offered me all the wealth in the world I could not develop an algorithm in a month of Sundays. But I do have a deep knowledge and understanding of marketing—and computer scientists would do well to follow my lead with regard to their area of expertise and accept/recognize/appreciate that

effective marketing is no easy task for those without the natural incli-
nation, education, and experience.[1] As I have said so many times, to so
many people, in so many places: if marketing is so easy why do so many
organizations, brands, and products get it wrong so often? On the positive side, however—there will always be work for the likes of me putting
right the mistakes made by these Jonny-come-latelies who think they are
marketing gurus because they can spell *Google*. Author's rant over.

A footnote to this section is that while I am of the same mind as Seth
Godin (2007), who when referring to *digital* said: "New marketing isn't
about technology any more than fast food (and the drive-through window) is about cars," I also freely accept that too many of my marketing
colleagues have shown a particular aversion to learning the *very* basics of
digital technology that they need to know in order to practice or teach
contemporary marketing.

## 5.2 Who Does What, and When

Aligned to the issues raised in the previous section are the *shop-floor* operations required for effective social media marketing. Once again, there is
the conundrum of demarcation lines between strategic, operational, and
shop-floor functions. To get around this I'll lean on a standard cop-out
and say *it depends on the organization*—and I can say this because it is
true. In small businesses there tends to be very little distinction between
planning and implementation in all aspects of management, whereas the
larger the organization the more formalized the structure of operations
becomes. In keeping with the title of the section, let's consider issues
related to the who, the what, and the when of social media marketing.
The standard caveat applies in that they differ for every organization,
brand, or product.

Although some aspects of *shop-floor* social media marketing will be
reactive, the organization must also be proactive in developing content
for the various platforms. As anyone who has ever written—or tried to
write—a blog will testify, finding something that will interest the readers

---

[1] Yes, I do appreciate that there are exceptions to this rule, but they are few and
far between.

gets harder as the days go by. Therefore, having *creativity* in the team is essential, and while it would be great if you could employ the sharpest, the wittiest, the smartest staff, they are probably working elsewhere for more money—so you need some pre-prepared off-the-shelf comments, lines, responses, and so on. Not scripts. Scripts are for telesales—the merest whiff of a script on social media and you lose customers. But staff do need help. Give them phrases that they can put into their own words. Think of it as the witty retort to that comment in the bar—you know, the one you wish you'd thought of at the time and not an hour when you are at home.

There is also the subject of writing guides for staff—the house style. As with any professional publication, there has to be a style sheet. This *guide* includes anything and everything from opening salutation ("hi" ... given name or title?) to closing ("best wishes").[2] Simple? What if you trade internationally, or your customer base includes people from different religions or backgrounds? Aspects of syntax must also be agreed—again, consistency is the aim. Then there is spelling and grammar. It may well be that the audience could care less about spelling, or they may not even know what is correct and what isn't, but it should be correct. Correct, that is, with some leeway. Social media is informal, so some rules can be relaxed—I've even started some sentences with *and* in this book. I can feel the glare of my old English teacher even as I type. None of this is rocket science, but needs to be determined to ensure consistency. By this stage, let's assume that the font, color, size, etc. have all been programed in to the software, but even they should all have be discussed and decided by the marketing and social team, not left to the software programmers.

Which brings us to the thorny issue of editing? Does every Twitter reply or status update need to be *approved* with regard to the two key issues of:

- Suitability. Some of the most memorable tweets are those
  that react instantaneously to events or happenings. But then,

---

[2] For an example of not getting it right, see: http://www.getoutsidethebottle. blogspot.co.uk/2016/03/not-right-salutation-solution.html

some of the most memorable tweets are those in bad taste that reflected badly on the organization, brand, or product.

- Grammar and spelling. Do you only employ people with the necessary skills to self-edit? A good plan, but they may be thin on the ground, and so, expensive.

Any delay brought about by some kind of editorial *review* can reduce the impact of comments significantly—that's if you have an editor available 24/7/365. And let's not go down the "what does legal think of it?" route (see my comments on this issue in Chapter 4 (Section 4.5)). It is also the case that effective social media marketing will include repeating (e.g., re-tweeting) the content of other authors, organizations, news reports, and so on. Who makes the call on whether or not they are *right* for the social media presence of your organization, brand, or product? No one remembers the 999 times you got it right, they remember the once you got it wrong. On the other hand, there is time for pre-prepared content to go through this process, to get prose just right. But then, you should be employing a professional writer for this content, and they will know how to get thing *right*, which includes making the content part of a narrative between publisher and reader.

A related subject that might have been included in the strategic chapter is that of the organization's *social voice*. That is: the *tone* of *voice* that the product, brand, or organization will use throughout its social media presence. For ease of discussion, I will refer to this as the *voice*—though I do appreciate that other terms are equally valid. I have opted for it being in *operational* in that the strategic decision would be "to use social media as an aspect of our strategic marketing with the following objectives." How those objectives will be met effectively and efficiently are generally perceived as operational issues—albeit ones that might need strategic approval. Getting the *voice* right is vital as it reflects the very nature of social media—that it was not developed as a marketing platform, and users do not like it to be used a platform for marketing. Therefore the voice must be *social*. Any attempt at marketing, or corporate, speak will result in failure of the social media marketing effort.

Do you need a social media calendar? That I'm asking should suggest the answer is yes; issues to consider include:

- Planned marketing events, be they off or online. For example, expect more social media when a new TV ad airs.
- National—or international—events. Black Friday and the Super Bowl spring to mind. Commenting on his organization's preparation for his company's National Pancake Day, IHOP's Chief Marketing Officer Kirk Thompson described it as "executing and implementing a social media war room."
- Calendar events. In the UK more people shopped on mobile devices on Christmas Day 2016 than any other day of that year. I'll bet they also accessed the social media sites of many an organization, brand, or product.
- Seasons—we have four every year. Some posts are more suited to different weather conditions so planning ahead might be a good idea. And don't forget the climate on the West Coast differs from that on the East Coast—as do all the places in between.

It's not really part of the social media calendar, but staff take vacations, something to bear in mind for the things listed above. But wait, within the calendar there should also be the daily or weekly schedule. How many posts should be made on each of the platforms per day? Or per hour? What time is optimum for those posts? And don't forget that your 9 a.m. is not everyone's 9 a.m. Using tools such as Facebook Insights and Twitter Analytics (other third-party tools are out there), you can timetable content to be published when your audience is most likely to see it—with most platforms facilitating the scheduling of posts, so you don't have an alarm going off in the office to alert staff to *post now*. Inherent to all of the above is that social engagement is a two-way street, if a customer asks a question or makes a comment, to be effective—that is, to meet the customers' needs—the response must be as near as possible, immediate. As any manager in customer service will tell you, planning for customers' agendas isn't easy.

In this section I have deliberately concentrated on using social media marketing for *larger* organizations as it is easier to give examples of the operational issues. However, a great many owners and managers of *small* and *medium*-sized *businesses* (SMBs) find the lure of the King's New *Digital* Clothes overly tempting and embark on social media marketing without fully appreciating what is involved. Though neither is commercial (one is a hobby, the other required as an author) I have a blog and a Facebook page. On the blog I post entries as and when I come across stories I think are suitable. This may be every day or so or weeks might go by with nothing. The same can be said for my Facebook page where most of my followers are ex-students now working in digital marketing. For both, a key reason for a lack of postings is that—and this is significant—I might not have the time because I'm doing other things... like writing books. My ethos of "if it is worth doing it is worth doing well" (or at least as well as I am able) means that I treat each posting as a publication in my name. The draft(s) are prepared in a word document and the spelling checked. Very rarely does the first draft go out without some amendment. The syntax is often played with to get the voice is right. The nature of the platforms is that any images need to be optimized for the platform then saved on my PC before downloading. Then there's the title and first line: do they appeal enough to tempt the reader into looking at the whole thing? All this and I'm not too bad at writing and grammar, other people find them difficult. The point I am trying to make is that even the most basic blog entry or Facebook post takes time. I have the time because, well, I have the time. I do not run or manage a business. Oh, and I didn't post anything during my two-week summer vacation. If social media marketing were to take up only an hour of an SMB owner's time each week, that's an hour they are not doing whatever their business is. Economists call it a lost opportunity cost. OK, so there are exceptions. A cake decorator taking a quick photo of every completed cake and posting it on Pinterest isn't going to take much time. But how long will it be before followers get bored with half a dozen cake pictures every day? Ironically, small owner-managed businesses are often the ones that best reflect the culture—and very often, passion—of their owners and so are ideally suited to social media marketing, but they simply do not have the resources to undertake it not just properly, but properly every time.

## 5.3 Third Party Platforms

Before getting any further in this chapter, one thing needs to be made very clear. Facebook, Twitter, YouTube (owned by Google), Instagram,

Snapchat, LinkedIn (owned by Microsoft), Pinterest, et al. exist not to entertain the masses or provide a free communications platform for those masses. They exist to make money. It is necessary that social media marketers appreciate this from the get go. Furthermore, although they may appear to be supportive of, and helpful toward, organizations that use them, the social media platforms will always make decisions based on how well they can benefit their shareholders. Inevitably, this means income from advertising will rule—with the *social* part of social media taking a poor second place. Of course the platforms will do their best not to upset the public—after all, the produce-content-and-sell-advertising-around-it business model requires folk to visit the site in order for the publisher to sell that advertising. However, for the organization using the platform as part of its strategic marketing communications, the platform's profit-oriented changes may impact on that strategy—an issue covered later in the chapter.

### 5.3.1 Why Use Third-Party Platforms?

The simply answer to this is that your customers inhabit these platforms. They already live on the likes of Facebook and Twitter. The platforms are also free at the point of use—that is, there is no financial price to pay. That said, hosting your own social media marketing content can be a better option. In the case of a blog, for example—if it was on your own website domain then you get the double whammy of it bringing people to your site and the search engines would index the blogs. Similarly, a technical forum or after-sales social service might be best hosted on a website owned and published by the organization, brand, or product.

### 5.3.2 What Are the Drawbacks in Using Third-Party Platforms?

From a strategic standpoint, there is the issue that by using third-party platforms organizations are sending customers to the domain of another business. A business that may well carry adverts for their competitors. This would probably be filed under *it's a necessary evil* by most organizations, but consider that bastion of impartiality, the BBC, for example (in the UK, the BBC is paid for by householders buying TV licences—it is not commercial as it is elsewhere in the world. Neither does BBC.co.uk have any ads). Whereas newsreaders and announcers tread on eggshells to avoid giving reference to product or brand names, they readily end reports by telling (advertising?) that viewers can follow the story on Facebook and Twitter. This has been the norm for a number of years and so users are used to following the BBC on social media—but what if, for example, Twitter was bought by News Corp or Fox News? Furthermore, February 2017 saw the BBC announce that its Planet Earth II show was to be shown in the United States on BBC America—but with trailers on Snapchat. This BBC example is not the same as *The Washington Post* (and others) partnering up with Snapchat Discover—that is a commercial decision between business partners, with each benefiting equally from WaPo providing multiple news updates on the social media platform throughout the day. Similarly, in the United States, as presidential candidate and then as president elect, Donald Trump used Twitter extensively—which he had every right to do.

But when he became president is it right that he continued to use a *branded* media outlet? However, this is a tad harsh on President Trump; President Obama used the @POTUS Twitter handle when he was in office—which was, of course, handed over to Donald Trump upon his inauguration, marking the first Twitter transfer of power in U.S. history. The story doesn't end there, however. Followers of @POTUS were transferred over to Barack Obama's @POTUS44—or not, as the case may be. Many found that they had been accidently subscribed to Trump's tweets without their say so and complained long and hard—on Twitter, naturally.

At a similarly strategic level, what if you have invested time and resources into a presence on a platform and you wake up one morning to find that platform has closed down? Far-fetched? I present Vine as an example. Or Twitter's *Dashboard* that had its plug pulled in January 2017, only six months after the app aimed at helping businesses to manage Twitter accounts was launched. Competition is also rife in the platform marketplace. For example, since the launch of Snapchat, Facebook had been content to replicate the picture apps service, but December 2016 saw Facebook announce new camera tools for its Messenger app that suggest the social media giant is going after Snapchat's users, which might ultimately see us wave goodbye to what was a very innovative addition to social media. Also, as I write, Twitter is *still* up for sale. Will it close? I doubt it, but any buyer might change the way it operates.

Which brings us onto the fact that social media platforms have a *my house, my rules* hold over users—be they social users or business users. Changes that platforms make to their service are often to the advantage of the business user—essentially to keep them sweet—but even minor changes have to be tracked, analyzed, and evaluated by business users, with operating procedures changed accordingly. Some of these changes will be relatively minor (they seem to be announced on a weekly basis), but others might edge toward requiring strategic consideration. Facebook's *Live 360 Video* and Instagram's *Live Streaming* both being launched in at the end of 2016 are examples. Whether or not either service is relevant or useful to the organization, brand, or product, there has to be a conversation in order for that decision to be made. For example, early in 2017 TripAdvisor introduced an enhanced subscription service that gave hotel and restaurant owners greater control over review and photo presentation. So, for the social media marketers, a bit of extra work to be done—after the additional cost has been agreed by whoever holds the purse strings. Other changes—and who knows what might be round the social media corner—may be both unavoidable and create significant problems for social media marketers.

The best—or is that worst?—example of *my house, my rules* dates back to December 2013 when Facebook changed its *News Feed* algorithm. When this modification was examined by social media marketers they found that *organic* brand page reach had plunged from the Facebook's previously stated 16 percent to under 3 percent. In essence, this meant that a brand could expect to reach only three out of every hundred fans who had liked the brand's page instead of 16—enough to require a strategic re-think. Skeptical commentators were quick to point out that brands would be more likely to resort to Facebook's paid method of promoting new posts. Having engagement reduced by nearly 80 percent or going cap-in-hand to the CFO for some more budget to cover these costs over the previously free service is most certainly a strategic issue.

But what if Facebook should suddenly decide that access to it for users was no longer to be free? Fewer users equals fewer people to access a brand's Facebook pages. Never happen? In late July 2017 Facebook was confirmed to be in talks with several news publishers to begin testing a *paywall* for subscription news stories in fall of the same year. By the time you read this you may know more.

In summary: social media platforms exist to make money and their platforms are their houses—where they play by their rules. Social media marketers beware.

# CHAPTER 6

# Social Media Marketing: What Works, What Doesn't... and Why

*I never made a mistake in my life; at least, never one that I couldn't explain away afterwards*

## A review of some social media marketing—not quite *X-factor* feedback, but some opinionated content

I addressed the issue of organizational culture in Chapter 4 (Section 6), and ultimately the culture of the organization will play the key role in whether or not any social media marketing is successful. However, having the right culture is not a guarantee—all of the other elements of social media marketing covered in this book are important, and even the right organizations can make strategic or operational mistakes. Articles with titles like *10 tips for social media success* abound on the web, but I have yet to read one that even mentions having the right culture. It's rather like giving someone 10 tips for success as a stand-up comedian when that person has no sense of humor. He or she might be brilliant at other things, but you are either naturally funny, or you are not. Organizations are *naturally* suitable to succeed at social media marketing or they are not. No amount of tips will change that.

## 6.1 The Right Brand and/or Product?

I'll start this section with a little exercise that might give you a little insight into which products and services might benefit from social media marketing—it won't take you long.

List where you have spent money in a B2C scenario in the last week, last month, or last year (longer will represent a more valid piece of research) then put them into categories where social media marketing did or didn't play a role in your purchase decision-making process. If you are anything like me, it is with small to medium sized businesses where most of my purchases are made, although bigger value purchases tend to be with larger companies. To get you started, what about this prompt list based on my spending in the last week or so.

The local store where you picked up some milk, the gas station where you filled the car, the canteen at work, the vending machine outside your office, your local bar (or in my case, bars), the garden furniture you ordered from the mall, some stamps from the post office, a magazine, fruit and vegetables from the nearby fruit and vegetable shop, the Italian restaurant where you had the early-bird special, the car parts you ordered on eBay, the guy who cleans your house windows, the sandwich from a stand in the mall while you were shopping in your lunch break, the ticket for the soccer match (bought online, but not via social media), the car park for that match, the burger from the stand going into the stadium, ditto the pie on the way out but from a different seller, more gas—but different garage, groceries from a supermarket (let's not go into the individual products), the guy who washed your car in the supermarket car park, the special cleaner you needed for your kitchen floor tiles (researched on the web, but not social media), your physiotherapist, the slightly out-of-code chocolate bars from the little discount store next to your physiotherapist, your haircut, the car park at work (every day), some WD40 water-displacing spray (it comes of having an old car in the winter), the taxi that took you to the airport for a work trip abroad, the cafe in the airport, the sandwich to eat on the plane (a budget airline), the taxi from the airport at the destination, the well-deserved and much-needed beer at the hotel bar, the meal at the nearby restaurant (recommended by the hotel receptionist), the coffee and cake at a seafront cafe during an early morning walk—I could go on, but I'm sure you get the drift.

It's amazing where you spend your money when you write it all down—and a lot of it is spent with businesses that do not use social media for their marketing. Indeed, many of the retailers listed above do no marketing of any sort; ergo, they don't do any social media marketing.

There are a couple of caveats for this research: I don't do the social thing and so I admit that for some of the above I could have sought them out on a social media platform—the restaurant in the overseas trip, for example. However, if a friend recommended the restaurant to you on Facebook, that's social, but not marketing and if that restaurant has a social media presence but you didn't look at it means that its Facebook presence has not influenced your buying decision. It might even mean the restaurant's owner has bought into the Emperor's New *Digital* Clothes.

Some brands and products lend themselves to social media market-ing—particularly if the brand is a person. Sports personalities, media personalities, indeed any personality—provided, of course, they have some kind of distinctive personality. Indeed, anything or anybody that has fans is in the running for successful social media marketing—by defi-nition fans are fanatic, and they're referred to as such for a reason. I'm not a devotee of the term, but *lifestyle* brands or products naturally attract followers as they see themselves as part of that lifestyle's community—fitness, beauty, and anything related to fashion would be examples. Stella McCartney and Alexander McQueen spring to mind in that they com-bine personality, brand, and lifestyle products. They also lend themselves to image-based social media marketing. I note they both have over three million followers on Instagram.

I'm sure that without too much effort, I could have devoted a chapter to a certain Donald John Trump (the book of *Trump on Social* must surely be out by the time this one hits the shelves). In the previous chapter I mentioned Donald Trump's use of social media. Politicians are a good illustration in the issue of being *right* for social media marketing. For some it is a natural extension of their personality; for others it is alien to them. Like him or not, Donald Trump has personality. In the time that elapsed between me signing the contract to write this book and its first draft going to the publishers he went from Mr Trump, to President-elect Trump to President Trump—and not without significant help from his use of social media. When—shortly after his inauguration—President Trump named Neil Gorsuch as the person to fill a then vacant U.S. Supreme Court spot, not only did he eschew the standard news conference in the White House for making the announcement on Facebook Live, but promoted it earlier on his personal Twitter account, @realDonaldTrump (not @POTUS).

Movies, particularly if they relate to a genre or franchise, have obvious potential for social media marketing. Indeed, social media is a staple of movie franchise marketing as it ticks so many boxes. However, the social media success of many movies is social and not marketing. It is also the case that hit movie *Snakes on a Plane's* makers' brilliant use (manipulation?) of social media and citizen marketing was something of a one-off that would be difficult to reproduce. TV shows, particularly reality shows or anything with any ongoing storylines that can be discussed by viewers, are also prime candidates for social media marketing.

However, it is worth pointing out that social media marketing content for the likes of movies and TV shows is pretty much self-generating; you do not need to commission videos, for example, you just take clips from the productions. Similarly, the stars will have contractual obligations to do *to camera* pieces for publicity purposes, which can be used on social media. Add in the fact that the stars themselves will have their own social media presence and followers and you have the situation where social media marketing might—almost—be enough to publicize a new movie.

A caveat to this is that not all stars act responsibly on their own social media sites, with the obvious impact on their employers. Movie and TV studios will monitor social media for this reason. Worst case scenarios see contracted actors lose their jobs following ill-conceived social media posts. An example of this from the UK was Marc Anwar, a star of the classic soap opera *Coronation Street*, who was sacked for allegedly making racially offensive tweets about Indian people. That the Pakistan-born actor's Tweets referred to Indian people as "b*******" and "p***-drinking c****" can't have helped his case much. Note that in the actually tweets the offensive words were spelled out in full.

Sports stars too can fail to toe the social line. After a series of poorly considered social media comments about New England Patriots' quarterback Tom Brady's wife upon his return to the game after suspension following his trial for domestic abuse, NFL star Greg Hardy tweeted his regret for said posts. Given his history before, during, and after the trial there's little surprise that people didn't believe he was being genuine in his remorse.

A solution to such examples of the social media equivalent of foot-in-mouth syndrome is to employ a ghost writer—normally someone handling PR for the star, their employers, or their agent—to manage their social media accounts. Sadly, some clients need more managing than others. Being a highly paid star of soccer's English Premier League does not guarantee common sense, Sunderland's striker Victor Anichebe[1] being an example. The PR company acting for his agent should have checked that their client could cut and paste messages, for after a narrow defeat, Mr Anichebe received a message that said: "Can you tweet something like: Unbelievable support yesterday and great effort by the lads! Hard result to take! But we go again!" The trouble is that Mr Anichebe posted that message on Twitter verbatim. As Homer Simpson would say: D'oh! For fans it was simply confirmation that many highly paid sports stars care little for the supporters who shell out hard-earned cash to follow their team.

Any product that generated a cult like affection decades before the Internet was invented is always going to be a strong contender for being right for social media marketing. LEGO falls into that category. However, this is an example of the product—and its history—being spot on but the organizational culture taking a while to kick-in on social. Originally the building-brick manufacturer used social as a one-way media, relying— perhaps sensibly—on enthusiasts who formed their own communities. But the firm is nothing if not willing to learn (as its rather chequered business history attests) and the current social media offering is far more conversational in nature. Also of note, however, is that the company has harnessed its fans into its own-domain communities such as LEGO Ideas—including a forum for fans aged 13 years old and under to get together. As is stressed in Chapter 5 (Section 5.3), organizations, brands, and products are hostages to the fortune of the social platforms—host your communities yourself and that is not a worry.

Perhaps one of the best examples of how to use Facebook for effective social media marketing comes from a product that hardly leaps out at you as an obvious contender for success in any kind of marketing, let alone social. I refer to Flucamp—who carry out paid clinical medical trials. The company has got the social culture thing so right that their Facebook page goes beyond having the right voice, it actually has a personality of its own. There is some overtly promotional content, but it is the banter with users where it excels, with posters being treated as individuals with a mixture of humor, helpfulness, integrity, and candor.

---

[1] Mr Anichebe has since left the club.

The site is at its best when dealing with trolls, of which the company's service attracts many. From comments like "that's the best bit of sarcasm we've heard for a while sir, well played" to even more direct putdowns, it is the trolls who end up looking like the idiots that they are trying to make of Flucamp. Note this however. The staff working on Flucamp's social media are exceptional. Most definitely not someone drafted in on an internship or minimum wage. These people could be stars on broadcast media. I would wager that other organizations would pay them a lot of money to work on their social media, which means Flucamp will be fighting hard to keep them. Essentially, the whole thing hinges on these folk, without them—or others of the same calibre—that personality is lost. If anyone still thinks social media marketing is easy and/or cheap, I refer them to this example.

Almost the exact opposite of Flucamp, online/app-only Airbnb is a shoe-in for social media marketing success. However, October 2016 saw the home-stay network accused of having its user-interface block negative feedback from dissatisfied guests. Accident or design? Who knows, but the essence of social media is openness and honesty. Even if the faulty software was an oversight, trust is more easily lost than gained. That it came at the end of a troubled year for the company caused the story to garner more publicity than it might have done when Airbnb was still the darling of the digital world.

A cookie brand that everyone munched as a child—and maybe still does—might not need too much marketing (just get in the right place at the right price) let alone social media marketing. However, if you're reading this book you are probably aware of the Oreo 2103 Super Bowl tweet. If you don't know the story, simply type "Oreo Super Bowl tweet" into a search engine of your choice. It was very clever. It won awards. "Classic social media marketing" said the people who gave out the awards. But, (a) how many new customers did this tweet create, and/or (b) did it sell anymore cookies?

Niche products almost organically develop an enthusiastic following. The UK's Mutt Motorcycles do little by the way of advertising, word-of-mouth being sufficient to create demand for their small-engine 1960s Triumph dirt-racer look-alike motorbikes. But they do make a product for a small market, and as you might expect of a company named for a dog of mixed heritage, an owner called Cooter and a history of making chopper motorcycles, they have an ideal culture for social media marketing.

Word-of-mouth recommendations usually see potential customers arrive on the brand's Facebook page (Facebook.com/muttmotorcycles). As befits a small business, Cooter replies to all Facebook comments and questions himself, normally with a inkling of humor, but also sometimes with a *hint* of frustration. The cause of this irritation is one of the reasons that Facebook—or any social media platform—might not be ideal for online marketing. The offender is the Facebook Timeline. Spending a few minutes reading Mutt Motorcycles or any similar Facebook presence reveals a host of happy customers giving positive feedback, but these are alongside the brand's representative answering the same question over and over again. In Mutt's case, "how much do they cost?". There is not an easy solution, however, as although the bikes use a standard frame and engine, the rest is customized to the desire of the customer—so a price list is not really a viable solution.

Disclosure: I am a customer—the bike in Figure 6.1 is mine—and so authentic are they to the 1960s that they all exist only in black and white photos. However, I am going to add another social media marketing

*Figure 6.1  A Mutt 125 cc motorcycle*

question mark to this example. Not only is there the issue of Cooter answering the same question over and over, but the majority of Mutt's Facebook followers will come from one of two camps: (a) those like me who have already been *sold* on the idea of owning a Mutt, and (b) those who would love to own one but for a whole host of reasons never will. Their Facebook *like* is the 2017 eqivalent of the 1970s poster of a Lamborghini Countach on your bedroom wall. Realistically, if a *genuine* potential customer came across the Mutt Facebook page they have probably followed a link from somewhere (a friend who has seen it or owns a Mutt, maybe) and so already have an interest in making a purchase (in marketing, we call this process the *sales funnel*). A *genuine* potential customer would take a few minutes to investigate the product further rather than simply looking at a few photos on the Facebook. Scrolling down the Timeline or following the link to the company's website would be the obvious moves—either of which would have revealed the price, including more details of customization, delivery, local dealers, and so on. Any salespeople (particularly car or motorbike sales) reading this will appreciate my view on this—you soon learn to spot the *time waster* who is asking the price but will never buy; the first question genuine buyers ask is *not* the price—they probably already have a rough idea. In other words, for all Cooter's good social media marketing practice, the social media platform might not yield any sales. Is there a solution for Cooter—after all, as sales increase so does his committment to their manufacture and the business in general so his social media marketing time is limited? I would suggest developing the Facebook page so that it provides all the *asked-for* information—price, availability, and so on—with an invitation to follow the link to the businesses website. Other than the occasional glance to ensure things are OK, Cooter could more or less leave the Facebook page to those satisfied customers who want to comment on, or leave a picture of *their* Mutt (yes, mine's on there somewhere). A footnote to the Mutt story is that according to Sprout Social (2015) retailers failed to respond to more than 80 percent of consumer questions and requests on social media in 2015. I don't need to comment on these appalling statistics, do I? Let's hope they had gotten better by 2017—but I would not put money on it.

If Mutt Motorcycles is representative of the experiences of SMBs on social media, the following should also ring true to many such organizations. Again, this example is from my own consultancy files, and so must remain anonymous. This business is a small outdoor activity center with few staff—none of whom are designated as marketers. Essentially, the marketing is done by the owner/manager. Largely due to the age range of the users, she decided to follow the route of social media marketing—but with no specific objective for it. An existing member of staff was designated as *social media guy*, with another person being recruited to fulfil his existing *activity* duties. That was nearly 12 months prior to me coming across the organization. Sure enough, no direct income could be attributed to the social media efforts (predominantly, Facebook). Indeed, the owner's abiding memory of her social media endeavors was the problems caused by a wholly unwarranted complaint posted on the Facebook. After I introduced her to the Emperor's New *Digital* Clothes the owner changed her Facebook presence to a *home* page only with basic information and a link to the organization's comprehensive website. However, she followed this up with an at-the-center campaign encouraging customers to photograph themselves on the various activities and post them on personal social media pages—with the appropriate *tag* identifying the business and its location. The result was an increase in visitors to the website via social media (over the previous 12-month period of social media marketing) and the cost saving of the member of staff who reverted to his instructor role in his specialist activity. I have seen this low-commitment low-cost approach be equally successful for a Greek restaurant and a roadside diner—both of which rewarded customers who posted photos on social media with a lagniappe (I've been to N'Orleans. Twice).

A hardly scientific but very time-consuming meander around the social media presences of the UK's FTSE100 companies is quite revealing. As you would expect, representatives of certain industries have a significant social media presence as part of their B2C marketing—two prominent examples being Marks and Spencer PLC (retail) and the Burberry Group (luxury fashion house). I'll file those in my *right brand or product* group. More interesting, however, were the *corporate* social media offerings of those corporations that most of the general public have never heard of— but obviously have a major role to play in the economy of the nation. These include the likes of: British Land Company PLC and Schroder PLC (asset management), Glencore PLC (commodities producer and trader), and FMCG giant, Unilever. Naturally, these organizations are not obvious candidates for social media marketing (i.e., they do not really meet any of my *right* criteria; culture, brand/product, C-level support), but all seem to want to tick the social media marketing box and so have presences on one or more platforms. That my *right* concept might carry some validity is borne out by the low numbers of posts, followers, and engagement on these platforms. The majority of—and *all* in some instances—posts are made up of company news and updates, announcements, media coverage, and the like. My assumption is that the people who follow these organizations on social media are actually interested in these corporate announcements. Journalists, perhaps? Shareholders? Economics professors? Students with assignments? In the case of the 3,600,331 people who had liked Unilever's Facebook page they must wait with baited breath for the one or two posts the company puts out each month.

One of the world's leading brands with branches in just about every country and a history of environmental and societal commitment, McDonalds' culture should be perfect for social media and vice versa. However, in the autumn (it was a UK-centric campaign, but you can use *fall* if you wish) of 2015, McDonalds launched *Channel Us*, its own YouTube channel presented by popular YouTube personalities Gabriella Lindley and Oli White. However, only a year after the launch of what the fast-food giant described as "a ground-breaking moment for the brand in the UK" the channel was pulled. None of the "how to ... " videos—a staple of this kind of social media marketing—managed to make it to 1,000 views. So, if one of the world's major brands can't get social media video to work, can anyone? The answer probably lies somewhere in the fact that social media users aren't keen on social media being used for marketing. Maybe it's a UK thing, but compared to the number of customers who enter under the golden arches, McDonalds' UK Facebook and Twitter numbers are not really anything to write home about. However, when reflecting on the *Channel Us* closure, comments made by Ben Fox, head of media and customer engagement at McDonalds are particularly relevant to would-be social media marketers. He said: "We have learnt that content is really difficult and content with purpose is really important." Although one could argue that by October 2015 they should have researched social media marketing well enough to have already known that, but if McDonalds, with all its marketing might, experience and budget can't come up with social media content, then others should take note.

## 6.2 The Right Implementation—*What Could Possibly Go Wrong?*

The culture might be right; the product or brand might be right; but the implementation might be wrong. Alternatively, the *right* management and staff might just rescue *wrong* cultures or brands.

Research by business intelligence firm L2 (2017) offers an insight into what is happening in the world of social media marketing by reporting that although the percentage of brands that have a Snapchat account increased in 2016, many of the accounts lay dormant. The result of repeated sightings of the Emperor's New *Digital* Clothes perhaps?

Commenting on global events is seen as being good social media marketing. A joke is best if the news is lighthearted, but if the news is bad, respectful is the way to go. Therefore, if you are going to honor the passing of someone of note (2016 was a particularly bad year for celebrity deaths) decorum is the watch word. Well, at least you would think so, but that was not the case when pop star Prince died. Cheerios posted a memorial tweet. Nothing amiss with that, but unfortunately somebody in the brand's social media team thought that the *i* in *Rest in Peace* should have a small cheerio instead of a dot. Carrie Fisher, who as Princess Leia in the original *Star Wars* film wore a distinctive hair style, also passed away in 2016. Some wag at baked goods store Cinnabon decided that the Leia-haircut would look better if the side buns were replaced by Cinnabon rolls. So that was the image that accompanied the tweeted message: "RIP Carrie Fisher, you'll always have the best buns in the galaxy." In a similar vein, what was the social media team at Epicurious thinking of when they responded to the 2013 Boston Bombing with a tweet saying: "in honor of Boston and New England, may we suggest: whole-grain cranberry scones?" Likewise, at the height of Hurricane Sandy, Urban Outfitters declared that: "This storm blows (but free shipping Doesn't)! Today only." Naturally, the social-media sphere erupted at such crass attempts at squeezing a brand message out of someone's misery. I'm going to be generous and put the errors down to youthful ignorance and immaturity.

I'll bet the folk responsible—who are used to a flurry of not so politically correct personal texts arriving with in minutes of every celebrity death—did not even consider the possibility that what they were doing was insensitive, and not funny. Of course, if someone a tad more mature had held some kind of editorial role, things might have been different. A caveat to these—and hundreds of similar examples—is that I'm assuming the posts weren't deliberate. After all, some marketers will argue that any publicity is good publicity. I'm not one of them, but I do wonder if sales of Cinnabon rolls or Cheerios fell as a result of these incidents?

Editor please! Youthful innocence and lack of worldly experience was also probably to blame when online beauty magazine *Total Beauty* tweeting a message to Oprah Winfrey complimenting her on the tattoos made visible by her off-the-shoulder dress at the Oscar ceremony. No problem with that, you would think. Unless, of course, the tattooed star at the Oscars was actually Whoopi Goldberg. Don't expect the magazine to feature exclusive interviews from anyone who knows either lady in the near future.

Perhaps it is the *real time* nature of social media—and an attempt to meet that immediateness—that is the cause of gaffes such as these. Note that I say *cause*, not *excuse*. Such problems can be avoided if social media staff do not try to be funny and/or entertaining—just informal and helpful. Organizations using social media for customer support are one such example.

Editor please! You would think that *Super Hero* comics would be perfect for social media marketing—they tick so many boxes. But care is still required in the social media delivery. In an a attempt to catch up with rivals Marvel, DC Comics resorted to social media marketing for the Pakistani comics market—but it all went wrong when they posted a tweet that included a note that the English captions were all "Translated from the Pakistanian." Apart from there being no such thing as Pakistanian, the language of Pakistan is Urdu. I wonder what *Pakistanian* is for D'oh?

I'm including Dutch national airline KLM based on personal experience. I have flown with them a lot and get the feeling that the staff do care. However—in my experience—the opposite is true of KLM's partner Air France. This culture of service—or lack thereof—carries over to the two organization's social media where (almost) the same messages from Air

France do not seem as genuine as those from KLM. Maybe it's a Dutch/ French cultural thing? KLM uses a wide range of social media platforms, all with—it seems—different objectives. The KLM blog, which is hosted on its own domain, includes stories of the brand and seeks to develop a relationship with travelers. It is a similar story for Facebook, Instagram, Pinterest, Google+, and YouTube, though much of the content is featured on each. Twitter, however, is mainly for customer service and claims to answer every customer request within 17 minutes and update every five minutes. As is commonplace with similar organizations, and all major airlines, KLM also has an app that informs passengers of delays and such like. Their LinkedIn presence is a bit different though. It includes profiles of all KLM's employees—over 16,000 of them. Personal experience aside, KLM is generally recognized as one of the best exponents of social media in its marketing. This reputation is founded on the airline's use of social media during the 2010 *ash cloud* crisis—such use was far from common at that time. Speaking at the 2016 Festival of Marketing, KLM social media manager, Karlijn Vogel-Meijer, talked at length about the airline's social media strategy—including its *three pillar* strategy. Those pillars are: (1) Service, (2) Brand, and (3) Commerce. Replace commerce with income and pillar with objective and they should look familiar (hint: see section 4.2.1: Core Objectives to *Any* Internet Presence).

Editor and some kind of management please! On the subject of airlines: having a member of its staff post a pornographic picture as part of a tweeted message to a customer is bad enough. But the social team at U.S. Airways followed that up by accidentally copying the lewd photo into another tweet—which then went on to be seen by far more people than the original ever would have.

Editor please! In a response to the story of NFL star Ray Rice physically abusing his wife the hashtag #WhyIStayed was adopted by similarly abused women to tell their own stories. DiGiorno Pizza decided that "#WhyIStayed You had pizza" would help them sell more pizza. Why would they think that?

Online reviews can work—evidence suggests that they do—but here is another example of how so many organizations have been sold the Emperor's New *Digital* Clothes and decided that they should pursue reviews for every product they sell. I have received requests for a product review—along with rather syrupy "dear customer ... we value your opinion" dialog—for a household light bulb ("it lit up when I turned it on") and a car park ("I arrived. I parked. I left"). But really, what's to review?

Social media—or social media marketing? I'm putting on my *Mr Skeptical* hat for this example. In January 2017 creative communications student Eugen Merher from Germany became a viral sensation when his *Break Free* video went viral. The video was an assignment for his university course—and very good it is too. Like every such assignment submission of which its author is proud, the video was put on YouTube. Herr Merher also sent the video to Adidas. Again—my commercial contacts tell me— pretty much standard operating procedure for creative students. And so the video kicked around social media for a while until it became a story on Forbes and the Huffington Post. Then it *really* went viral. So was it social media—or social media marketing? Well, it went viral socially, that is; *organically*, so social media. However, when Eugen put it online and sent it to Adidas, wasn't he marketing himself? So social media *marketing*. Two caveats: (1) Millions of students' videos are posted online every year, but only this one went viral, and (2) this with my really skeptical hat on, might it turn out to be an Adidas sponsored campaign after all—you should know by the time this book is published.

Be careful what you ask for. Trusting the general public to toe the line with your social media campaign is always risky. The Natural Environment Research Council (NERC) thought they had a great *social* idea when they announced a campaign to name their new £200m Royal Research Ship with the hashtag #NameOurShip. Maybe you could put it down to that good old British humor—but even Monty Python would have been pleased to see the winner of the poll: Boaty McBoatface. An embarrassed NERC performed a quick soft-shoe shuffle and named the runner up as the chosen name. However, as a sop to enraged voters, the RRS Sir David Attenborough does carry an Autosub underwater vehicle called Boaty McBoatface.

What could possibly go wrong? In the UK, May 2017 saw brand leaders Walkers Crisps (that would be *chips* in the United States—it's one of those sidewalk-pavement, lift-elevator things) used their spokesperson, former soccer star and now TV pundit, Gary Lineker to front a social media-based campaign that encouraged users to add their *selfie* to a poster being held by Mr Lineker. However, the #WalkersWave campaign had to be pulled when pranksters added photos of mass murderers and convicted *celebrity* paedophiles to the poster. Bad taste certainly, but did no one at Walkers—or their agency—see this coming?

Social media is 24/7/365. The message on the Facebook homepage of a university not a million miles from me reads: "This page is monitored Monday - Friday 9am - 5pm. Spam and abusive posts will be deleted." So, if you want some abuse to get maximum exposure, around five past five on a Friday evening is your best bet. More concerning is that the message tells potential students that no one will answer your Facebook query outside office hours. Sadly, this is not an uncommon state of affairs in the *always-on* digital environment. As Levine, Locke, Searls, and Weinberger suggested—with commendable foresight—in 1999, "engagement in these open free-wheeling exchanges isn't optional. It's a prerequisite to having a future. Silence is fatal."

Editor and some kind of management please! It is beyond me why such things even get written, as a joke or otherwise: but somebody in the social media team of the New England Patriots (that would be the reigning Super Bowl champions, not some back-woods local team) mocked up an image of the team's shirt with a racially insulting message and term where the player's name would be. In the UK at least, that's a sackable—and probably criminal—offense in itself. But even worse, the image and hashtag were used in a tweet to thank fans for bringing the team's Twitter feed numbers up to a million. Having some numbskull in the social team making such a joke is one thing. Developing a message that automatically triggered when the one millionth person signed on—sometime in the future—without checking that message is unforgivable. I refer you back to Chapter 5 (Section 5.1) where management and staffing is addressed. I'm guessing that many of the *errors in judgment* featured in this chapter came about as the direct result of someone being given a job they should not really have even got the interview for.

On the subject of teenagers—if many of the guilty parties featured here are not teenagers, they think like they are teenagers—here's a misguided attempt to woo those child-adults in that awkward 11- to 15-year-old age group. I have always said that marketing to teenagers is difficult because they live in a world of their own and marketers are no longer teenagers—but they can remember when they were. Such is the nature of teenage years, however, that there are 10 different *teenage years* every decade. It's a bit like dad-dancing at weddings, no teenager wants to associate with anything grownups think is cool, or more to the point what grownups thought was cool when they were teenagers. And the reason I mention this is a campaign from Reese's chocolate bars, and as a preface to the story I should mention they are not a big seller in the UK. Carrying the strapline #Sorrynotsorry, the Hershey Company's first-ever UK-specific social media campaign for its Reese's confectionary brand was aimed at millennials but managed to present an image of young people that most millennials didn't recognize. Postscript: this is one reason why teenage bloggers have become so popular with teenagers *and* why they are excellent conduits—as influencers—to teenagers for social media marketers.

In Brazil, Uruguay, Chile, and Argentina, Hellman's mayonnaise used WhatsApp to offer users advice on what meal that could make from what they had in their refrigerator by taking a snap of the contents. *WhatsCook* chefs then offered tips and advice on what could be made with the ingredients. Nice idea, but limited longevity—and how many chefs do you need on call to keep up with demand. Perhaps it is only meant as a *flash in the pan*? (thank you, I'm here all week). Check if the promotion is still available when you read this.

Staff training please! "Hey, I only crunch the numbers" would have been no excuse for Twitter's chief financial officer, Anthony Noto, when he didn't seem to realize how Twitter worked and accidently tweeted a message about a forthcoming buyout discussion. That the tweet read "I think we should buy them" will have given the prospective seller a certain edge in negotiations.

Social media marketing has become a popular option for restaurants—fast food or otherwise—and they have taken to *social* in a big way. Among many other examples of so-called *food stunts*, 2016/17 saw:

- Wendy's created a mock news station on Tumblr and YouTube stories as part of the launch of additions to its 4 for $4 menu.

- Denny's used custom Snapchat filters and Facebook Live events to promote their new buttermilk pancakes.
- As part of its National Cheese Toast Day (there's nothing like inventing a *your product day* to promote your product), Sizzler invited fans to create personalized memes depicting how the dish makes them feel—obviously the content is designed to be shared. In addition, there was a best *selfie* featuring cheese toast completion.
- Denny's tweeted for followers to zoom in on a photo of the brand's iconic pancake stack, which led them on a tour of the image from the syrup round each corner and back to the butter—and a special message. In less than 24 hours of being posted the tweet generated 1,600 replies, 84,000 *retweets*, and 114,000 *likes*, making it Denny's most popular tweet of all time.

For all of these the objective was to increase engagement, and I can see how they might, but only among existing customers. Who else would have connected with the restaurants on social media platforms? And who worked out the ROI? I wonder if lower prices, a discount coupon, or better service might have been preferable to the majority of customers who did not *engage* in these events?

A similar issue of who but existing customers bought the promoted product can be seen in a Starbucks campaign in April 2017 when the coffee giant had a limited-run *Unicorn* Frappuccino promotion that caused a stir on the main social media platforms, but mainly Instagram—a point that is relevant as the product's pink and blue color lent itself to images rather than textual descriptions. The social media driven campaign resulted in massive sales of the Frappuccino—much to the chagrin of the baristas who complained about how it stained their hands and was complicated to make, so disrupting work flows for the five-day promotion. The disgruntled staff let the world know of their problems—on social media, naturally. So, on the face of it—staff relations apart—a successful promotion. But did it get any ROI? Did anyone who wasn't already a *friend*—that is, a customer—see the promotion on social media and rush to a cafe to buy one? Or was it existing customers who replaced their normal order with a *Unicorn* Frappuccino?

Someone at tablet manufacturer Razor thought that a play on words would be funny. And it can be, so long as the play doesn't take you from a perfectly acceptable meaning to one that is sexually explicit. In a 2016 Twitter campaign, Razor wanted to bring attention to their product having a secure digital (SD) slot whereas their main competitor—the Mac-Book Pro—doesn't. The Razor tweet read: "You call yourself Pro? S my D." I'm going to say I can make a very good guess at the age and gender of the person who came up with masterly double entendre. I'm also obviously not in their target market as I actually had to look up the term that caused offense. Although the company quickly deleted the offending post and tweeted an apology ("to those who were offended, it was intended as a light hearted turn of phrase that missed the mark") the irony is that the tweet got nearly 5,000 likes, suggesting that the target customer base found it funny. Which is exactly what effectively segmentation and target marketing is all about (if you deliberately appeal to one group you do not appeal to others), and that's why I'm putting it in the *successful* social media marketing column—the apology wasn't for the real customers. Indeed, I'll give Razor the benefit of the doubt and say the whole thing was designed to create publicity through controversy, and I doubt it has cost many—if any—sales. It will certainly have raised the organization's social credibility to those young men playing MMOGs with their baseball caps on back-to-front and slurping energy drinks.

Blackberry saw its star wane from leader of the mobile pack to also-ran as smartphone popularity grew. There is a certain irony, therefore, that when the organization tweeted a picture of its new smartphone the tweet carried the footer message that it has been sent from an iPhone. But this example gets worse, this time for smartphone maker LG. Their French social media team (who obviously do not keep up with social media marketing good/bad practice) mocked Apple's problems with their bend-and-break iPhone 6—in a tweet also sent from an iPhone. Do'h!

One thing that has gained prominence since Mr Trump made it to Pennsylvania Ave is the question of a re-tweet being an endorsement. The issue has always been around—and could apply to all re-sent messages on any platform. However, a number of folk who re-tweeted anti-Trump messages prior to polling day have now seen which side of their bread is buttered and turned Trump supporter, prompting the search through their social media history. So, if you re-tweet a message is that a sign that you support the message. Of course it is—unless you are being ironic, which is a hard sell when the press start digging into your social media past.

Social service—or social publicity generator? In August 2016, Marriott International announced the launch of its M Live Europe, the Company's Fourth Global Marketing Real-Time Command Centre. According to Marriott's press release:

> M Live empowers Marriott to interact with guests in a more per-sonalized way and participate in one-to-one conversations on social platforms where travellers are already actively engaged. It tracks conversations, trends, global performance, marketing cam-paigns and brand reputation across social platforms in real-time, identifying opportunities for Marriott to engage consumers with its 19 brands and nearly 4,500 properties worldwide.

That sounds impressive, and more so when the press release went on to quote vice president of global creative and content marketing, David Beebe, saying: "We created M Live with an understanding that real-time marketing always starts with the guest, and the best way to engage with consumers is to start a two-way conversation that is relevant to their needs and preferences as travellers." The press release goes on to give a couple of examples of how guests' stays had been enhanced by the *Global Mar-keting Real-Time Command Centre* (is it just me, or does that sound like something from a *Saturday Night Live* spoof of Thunderbird's Marketing Island?). By *enhanced*, read *compted*—Marriott Rewards points for one, a free stay for another. As you might expect, recipients of such gifts were quick to talk about it on social media. I have a couple of points: (a) the recipients of Marriott's real-time service are identified by "geo-fencing technology" (software that uses global positioning system—GPS—or radio frequency identification (RFID) to identify where a user is); plenty of organizations use this, but it is a bit spooky, and (b) how long before it is common practice to tweet something like: "I'm staying the Marri-ott *anytown* and really disappointed with the meal in the restaurant" or "the next stop on my charity tour of Greece is Athens—haven't booked a hotel yet" hoping that Marriott's social media team pick it up? From a business perspective—and I know software is available to support them—how many multilingual staff does it take to run each of these *Command Centres* 24/7/365? And don't forget the proposition is to not only enhance the service offered to guests at the Marriott's 19 brands and around four and a half thousand hotels worldwide, but *potential* customers who might be writing on social media about where they are on holiday. So, social service—or social publicity generator? Checking if M Live is still, well, *live* might help you decide.

A final example for this section was brought to my attention during an exercise in one of my classes. I'll refrain from naming the company, but it is a significant player in UK e-commerce. The range of products sold—which includes many brand names—would put them in the retail category of *department store*. On Facebook the company is *liked* by 463,490 people and *followed* by 437,620. The Facebook *home* page carries the message: "like us & we promise we'll love you by keeping you up to date on the latest trends, news & exclusive competitions!" I think it is a rational assumption that this organization has a significant investment in social media marketing. My audit of their Facebook *Timeline* over a 14-day period in February 2017—which included Valentine's Day—is as follows:

- An average of five posts per day, all of which were for products or product ranges accompanied by introductions like "weekend casual chic!," "Give your outfit some attitude," and "Pink to make the boys wink!" As these sample introductions suggest, the majority of posts were for female clothes and accessories—this despite the website offering men's clothes, electrics, and home and garden products.
- There was no content encouraging social engagement.
- There was an average of 17 *likes* per post with a rather miserly total of 21 comments and 3 shares for *all* 70 posts.
- In the same way as any research should discount any data that is extreme when compared to the norm, I have not included the following in these figures:

- One post that included a competition received 136 entries (comments) and 39 shares.
- Another post—for reasons that were not obvious—received 1.2 thousand likes, 30 comments, and 16 shares.

However, out there for everyone to see was a total of 29 complaints from customers, which included the following comments:

- Just don't expect the order to be correct, or get anywhere with their appalling customer service…
- I will not be ordering from this company again, it's great it you can do it all on line but you cannot get speak to anyone. The customer services dept is a joke.
- I can honestly say i will not be ordered any electrical products ever again…
- Do you sell seconds.. My girlfriend got me a LG mobile phone off you and its absolutely terrible.
- Highly recommended; do check out Visitor posts and feedback on here before you purchase!
- Once orders are placed … From that moment on this company does NOT care to sort problems out and often don't even apply the codes that we are given for a discount.
- Completely ripped me off.
- Your call centre staff are rude and hang up on customers rather than dealing with issues.
- Still no reply from customer services. 4 forms filled in and nothing.
- I have experienced the worst customer service with Very of any company I have ever dealt with.

No matter how much—or how little—investment the company makes on its social media marketing, I would suggest that comments such as these are a good reason for reducing that investment to *nil*. Add into the equation that realistically the customer engagement is negligible and an outsider looking in—as were my students—might propose that the cost of social media marketing might be better spent on improving their customer service. Sadly, even a cursory analysis of the social media presences of many e-commerce companies suggests that while my sample company's poor social media behavior is not the norm, it is far from being a one-off occurrence.

A last word on poor management and practice. Research published by BBDO Worldwide (Mullally and Lalji 2016) found that 97 percent of the top brands on Facebook were *still* using the organic posting model as a social strategy nearly three years after the platform changed its distribution algorithm (see Chapter 5 (Section 5.3)). That the change significantly reduced the reach of posts without opting for paid distribution suggests that the vast majority of social media marketers do not understand the industry in which they are working. Too busy taking *selfies* wearing their Emperor's New *Digital* Clothes perhaps?

## 6.3 The Right Culture?

The issue of organizational culture was addressed in Chapter 4 (Section 4.6), and ultimately the culture of the organization will play the key role in whether any social media marketing is successful or not. Take note, however, having only the right culture is not a guarantee—all the other elements of social media marketing covered in this book are important, and even the right organizations can make strategic or operational mistakes.

Elon Musk is not your average car company CEO. Actually, he's not your average businessman. He's different. He's outgoing. He's *right* for social media—and he knows how it works. His Twitter account has more followers than Ford, Chrysler, and Chevrolet combined. He even has more followers than his Tesla car—a product that is *right* for social media if ever there was one. He is, however, the exception to the rule. CEOs should venture onto social media with great care—and not without some sort of plan. Bosses look sillier than most when caught wearing the Emperor's New *Digital* Clothes.

"Silence is Golden" sang the Four Seasons back in 1964, and it can be very good advice for anyone representing an organization, brand, or product on social media, and here's an example. San Francisco's public rail service Bay Area Rapid Transit (BART) has seen a significant rise in demand due mainly to the technology-driven Bay Area economy. Sadly, BART's been struggling with budget problems for a number of years and the service's infrastructure is not up to handling the increase in travelers. As you might expect, frustrated customers regularly take to the organization's Twitter account to vent their spleen. And it was in response to one such negative comment that BART's twitter person—one Taylor Huckaby—was rather candid in his response. Shooting directly from the lip, he retorted: "BART was built to transport far fewer people, and much of our system has reached the end of its useful life. This is our reality." While some BART-using twitterers backed the honesty, far more did not. My opinion is that BART should not have touched social media with a barge pole. Trying to engage with a totally dissatisfied customer base is always going to be a lose/lose situation and this is an example of an unsuited organization jumping on the social media bandwagon without asking where that bandwagon would take them.

With the financial crisis—that would be the one generally blamed on the banking institutions—still impacting on millions of citizens, someone at J.P. Morgan came up with the idea of using (what they probably called) that intersociallytwitbookwebthingy to quieten the masses and show how hip they were. So the banking giant posted a tweet saying that following day the vice chairman would answer any questions posted on their Twitter page. Cue mass abuse from the social community and the cancelation of the Q&A event.

As a rule-of-thumb for would-be social media marketers, consider this: if the organization has a history of paying below minimum low wage; cutting costs on its staff welfare; had its tax returns questioned; ignoring environmental issues; poor press relations—or anything similar—then I cannot imagine it having the right culture for social media marketing. However, some brands with this sort of problem in their past have given it a go, only to realize that their own social media pages are an ideal forum for that past to rear its ugly head in the posts of folk with long memories.

Presumably, brand engagement was the objective for Nissan's *Diehard Fan* app, and in 2015 it saw 500,000 downloads generate over three million photos of users *virtually* painting their faces in their college football team's colors. No wonder then, that the campaign was repeated in 2016. Plenty of downloads and snaps? Tick. Generate brand awareness? You might need to ask all the users which brand was sponsoring the app before ticking that box. Sell more Nissan trucks? You decide. This is an example of an organization that is *playing* with social media, but does it have the *right* culture? The campaign might have been successful in the number of folks who downloaded the app, but if it didn't sell any trucks there was no ROI, unless you count as *returns* the thanks of thousands of face-painted students who have probably forgotten who it was that gave them the free app.

If ever there was a brand that was made for social media it is Virgin Airlines (in any of its guises). From the mid-80s when Virgin Atlantic launched, Virgin has been the epitome of everything that makes an organization *right* for social media marketing. The entire *corporate* culture revolves around giving the customer the best experience possible—and doing so with a smile on its face. Examples abound, but for an introduction to Virgin's social media marketing take a look at their BLAH airlines (put the name into a search engine) campaign, which includes a six-hour (yep, 6 hours) YouTube video. Do I need to add that the culture of the organization derives from its founder, Sir Richard Branson who is not one to be shy and retiring where PR is concerned.

Family restaurant chain IHOP has over three and a half million Facebook fans, so I'm going to put that in the *successful social media marketer* category. However, IHOP had a social program before the Internet was invented. It did so because of the culture of the organization. Take a look at "our philosophy" on the firm's website. It includes: "Everyday life has enough rules. Sitting down for a delicious, comforting meal shouldn't have any," "No need to dress to impress," and "Texting is no match for actual talking. Especially when it's over a fresh cup of coffee." A couple of years ago, for an April Fool's Day gag, they posted on Facebook a picture of a bacon dispenser sitting on the table. Not taking yourself too seriously is almost a prerequisite for effective social media marketing. In an interview the CMO, Kirk Thompson is reported to have said: "I have truly the best job in the world because I get every day to wake up and to think about pancakes, and fun." Note the last two words. OK, so it might have been rhetoric, but it rings true. IHOP is *right* for social media marketing.

Purveyors of outdoor clothing, Moosejaw, is another natural for social media. Any firm that decorates the rear door of their delivery trucks with the message: "Driver carries less than $50 cash and is fully naked" has got to be able to carry that culture onto social media. In an interview,[2] Moosejaw's CEO Eoin Comerford is quoted as saying: "we'll hire someone who is engaging and fun ahead of someone with actual retail experience." That has a familiar ring to my comments in the previous chapter with regard to recruiting the right staff. I should also add that the nature of the product range probably attracts the kind of both staff and customer who appreciate this culture.

Another company with the *right* culture is Zappos. Need I go on? You will be aware of the company not just as an exemplar of e-commerce practice, but of how to run a business. However, in social media where the brand excels is the way it uses video. From pranks through product information to support of Veterans, Zappos films it and puts it out on social platforms. This practice needs to be undertaken with care however. As all the videoed events are staged, this can lead to accusations of a kind of sensationalism. The practice of staged events is nothing new—I described them as *staged viral* a decade ago (a long time in social), using one classic example of a viral success as such. This was actor *William Shatner's* auction of his kidney stone at Las Vegas casino in 2006. It was for charity, so no-harm no-foul—but it was an obvious publicity stunt designed to take advantage of digital communications. Zappos has been astute enough to not be perceived as manufacturing events purely for the YouTube video— their commitment to Veterans, for example, is genuine—but it would be an easy trap for a not so culturally *right* organization to fall into. On social media fakes are easily recognized and summarily *outed*.

In my experience there is not a single UK university that has the *right* culture for using social media as a tool for marketing—furthermore, my own research suggests that universities' social media plays only a bit part in students' decision-making process for choosing which university to attend. Note that I emphasize the universities' social media, which does not include the likes of Facebook pages produced and maintained by students or student clubs and societies. The vice chancellors—they are the CEOs in UK universities—are products of the system they oversee, with

---

[2] https://econsultancy.com/blog/65437-how-moosejaw-s-tone-of-voice-creates-hilarious-multichannel-experiences

academic integrity ruling above just about everything. It is not a place for brevity. It is not a place for the kind of culture in which social media marketing thrives. I suspect the same can be said of European universities. Having done some research into the websites of U.S. universities, the content on those gives me reason to assume that the same can be said of them. A caveat is that in the U.S. universities are businesses as much as they are educational establishments, and so there may be some stakeholders of a university somewhere that have bought into a Zappos/Virgin/IHOP philosophy—if there is let me know, it must be a great place to study or work.

Whenever I teach the *consumer reviews* element of social media marketing I use a hotel case study and always end the class by asking the question: "what is the best way to always get positive reviews?" The answer—of course—is to always provide a product or service that exceeds the customers' expectations. It would seem that the owners of the Union Street Guest House in Hudson, NY, were not on the same customer service page as me with their review policy, which read:

> If you have booked the Inn for a wedding or other type of event anywhere in the region and given us a deposit of any kind for guests to stay at USGH there will be a $500 fine that will be deducted from your deposit for every negative review of USGH placed on any internet site by anyone in your party and/or attending your wedding or event. If you stay here to attend a wedding anywhere in the area and leave us a negative review on any internet site you agree to a $500 fine for each negative review.

As you would expect on social media, the policy went viral—aided and abetted by the *New York Post* giving it a mention. The hotel, it would appear, has since closed. I wonder why? The message for businesses that rely on reviews—and the hospitality industry is the obvious example—is "think before you act," and maybe take some advice also. The irony of this story is that it seems the hotel was actually very good.

Picture the scene: at the New York Police Department's PR meeting someone suggests that to improve the department's image they should run a social media campaign encouraging users to tweet photos featuring members of the NYPD. Everyone in the meeting must have thought: helping old folk across the road; directing tourists; catching bad guys. Showing people the Emperor's New *Digital* Clothes that were on show at NYPD headquarters? Really, did no one see the flaw in the plan and that not-quite-so-brand-enhancing pictures *might* also be posted? Or did no one want to speak out and be scorned as a fool?

The U.S. State Department = not the right culture. Why else would it send out a tweet to warn U.S. citizens traveling overseas to look out for ne'er-do-wells that says: "Not a 10 in the U.S? Then not a 10 overseas. Beware of being lured into buying expensive drinks or worse—being robbed." In a similar vein to the teenager issue mentioned earlier in the chapter, I have visions of this idea coming from a 50-year-old bloke wearing a baseball hat on backwards. And chinos.

Sometimes culture can translate as personality. One restaurant that did not come out well (do any?) in an episode of the TV show *Gordon Ramsay's Kitchen Nightmares* was Amy's Baking in Scottsdale, AZ. So bad was the place that Chef Ramsay left before filming ended. As is the case with all *reality* shows, social media was filled with chatter and comments. As can be expected the owners, Samy and Amy Bouzaglo, did not come out well. Rather than taking cover and letting the coverage pass, Mrs Bouzaglo made the decision to put her head above the Facebook parapet to respond. Opening with "most of you are fat, disgusting losers," she went on to let the world know that "my husband and I enjoy the finest chamagne (sic) and caviar whenever we so choose" and "you are disgusting pig people, made from the slime of your own hatred at the world for making you disgusint (sic) people" (note that in the original, the message was in uppercase). I haven't seen the show, but their social media response suggests that the celebrity chef had a point.

Innocent Drinks is another company that social media was made for. Or was Innocent another brand made for social media? Messages on its product's packaging that offers "rules for riding a dinosaur" and "contact via banana phone" projects a public image that cannot be anything but a reflection of the organization's underlying culture. Innocent had a cult following from its launch—indeed, that following was how it became successful; buyers took to the *zany* culture that was a million miles from other players in the drinks industry. That the cult following naturally moved to social media is no surprise. However, the brand uses social as an entertainment media more than a sales vehicle—which is exactly as it should be.

Any organization that uses a banner ad that says "Last one to sign up for a Paddy Power account is a twat" has got to be in the frame for being *right* for social media marketing. The tone of voice, in particular, is spot on. Paddy Power is a UK[3] off and online betting company that has nearly a million and a half likes on Facebook and over half a million followers on Twitter. Neither are they afraid to take a dig at other brands. In June 2017 an investigation by the BBC's Watchdog program found that samples of iced drinks from Costa Coffee, Starbucks, and Caffe Nero contained varying levels of the bacteria from faeces. Several of the said brand's coffee outlets were unfortunate to be located next to PaddyPower shops—which posted signs in their windows that read: "Don't gamble next door … we won't sh*t in your coffee." Very unpolitically correct in nature, the company's tone of voice is *men at the pub*, but it has some very witty and astute writers. Add this to the access to sports stars any sports betting company has and you also have jokes and pranks at the expense of famous soccer players and athletes from a range of sports. Importantly, it never takes itself very seriously, with gags often at the expense of the social media writers. Paddy Power is another perfect example of segmentation—where the *right* message to the *right* segment is effective, but to another segment the same message just doesn't work—and will turn that segment away from the product. However, so entertaining is the content that industry insiders reckon that over half of Paddy Power's likes and followers are not, and never will be, gamblers. For their marketers then, is raising your brand profile among non-customers worth the effort?

As a nation, Austria must be low down on most folk's list of most entertaining nationalities—but the culture of energy drink Red Bull is a tremendous match with social media marketing. Add into the mix that as well as sponsoring popular sports like soccer and Formula One racing, the *niche* sports—for example, mountain biking, BMX, motocross, windsurfing, snowboarding, skateboarding, kayaking, wakeboarding, cliff-diving,

---

[3] Like many similar European organizations, for gambling license reasons, Paddy Power is registered *offshore* on the Mediterranean island of Malta.

parkour, and surfing—that Red Bull sponsor have loyal followers and we have a perfect match. Note that Red Bull is also a textbook example of a brand that is using synchronized multi-channel marketing. The sponsorship—and filming—of *skydiver* Felix Baumgartner's longest free fall parachute jump becoming a YouTube sensation being an example. Indeed, Red Bull's use of sponsorship, sports, events, celebrity endorsements, visual content, and storytelling—and a mix of them all on various platforms—makes them masters of social media marketing.

Although I have finished the chapter on a high with the Red Bull example of social media marketing excellence, I'll end it with the type of footnote that you should be used to by this stage of the book. To achieve that excellence, just how high is Red Bull's marketing budget? Probably somewhere up there with Herr Baumgartner.

# CHAPTER 7

# Conclusion

*I keep six honest serving men (they taught me all I knew); Their names are What and Why and When and How and Where and Who*

## 7.1 Ticking the Marketing Boxes

When it comes to social media marketing, too many organizations do little more than tick the boxes in the check list they found in some book or guru's website. The problem with check-box lists is that once the box has a tick in it, senior management pats itself on the back and proclaims to anyone who will listen that they have *managed* all of these boxes being checked—but they don't really care if each job has been done *effectively*. To do so might be to uncover the fact that they have actually managed nothing. It is this kind of strategic management that gives rise to the parable of the Emperor's New Clothes moving into the digital age. CEOs who do not ask questions can be easily fooled by the bright lights and press coverage of that social media phenomenon everyone is talking about as the panacea to all marketing ills.

*Open Facebook account* ✔
*Open Twitter account* ✔
*Hold Press Conference* ✔
*Pat self on back* ✔

-------------------------------------

*Identify SM objectives* ✘
*Calculate ROI* ✘
*Identify needs of customers* ✘
*Allocate budget* ✘
*Allocate resources* ✘
*Select appropriate platforms* ✘
*Recruit staff* ✘

*Complement the Emperor on his new clothes* ✔ ✔ ✔

So why have so many people bought into the Emperor's New *Digital* Clothes? Why have so many owners, CEOs, CMOs, and managers acted so irrationally in agreeing to spend money without a second thought for any return on investment? At risk of overdoing the metaphors in a book whose title is a folk-tale—there are none so blind as those that will not see. Furthermore, they do not know *what* they are supposed to be seeing. Therefore, it is no surprise when they *perceive* how well it works when shown it by its evangelists—because they do not actually know *what* social media marketing is. And therein lays the crux of the problem raised in the tale of the Emperor's New *Digital* Clothes.

Despite me offering up in this book a description of what social media marketing consists of, what it *actually* is eludes us. Social media is about sharing and engaging in communities and networks. Ergo, social media marketing must also embrace these characteristics. But so much of what we are told is successful social media marketing barely gives an acknowledging nod toward sharing or engaging. And here is the twist in this apocryphal tale. It would seem that most organizations now use social media platforms as *broadcast* media for content to be *pushed* out to the general public—the polar reverse of the ethos of social media.

This *broadcast* content is generally along the lines of information or news—with no attempt at any kind of engagement. So popular is this *social broadcasting* that younger audiences are more likely to view sports highlights on Snapchat or YouTube than they watch the full match or event on TV. Significantly, February 2017 saw an indicator of the way the future is shaping up when YouTube announced its $35-a-month YouTube TV with programing from some premium broadcasters including ABC, CBS, FOX, NBC, and ESPN, as well as well as live showings of NBA and MLB games. This was on top of a deal with broadcaster Univision to *livestream* matches from Mexico's top soccer division Liga MX. The same month saw—according to Twitter's CFO Antony Noto[1]—around 5.1 million people watching the Grammy's video content on Twitter during the awards show, with Noto going on to suggest that the company intended to double its livestreaming efforts in 2017. Around the same time the Google-owned video channel announced plans to run original programing on its YouTube kids app. Similarly, Facebook's plans to move away from *traditional* (it's only 10 years old, but so fast has it moved that it can be described as *traditional*) social media were betrayed by its

---

[1] Noto was speaking at the Goldman Technology Conference in San Francisco on February 15, 2017.

poaching one of YouTube's key music directors Tamara Hrivnak in January 2017—surely a declaration of intent for the social media giant.[2]

None of this content has any intent to *share* or *engage*—so it can't be considered part of social media *marketing*: can it? But if it is not part of social media, what it is part of? Social public relations? Social news? Social information? Social dissemination? Social notices? Social broadcasting? I like the latter as it best describes what is taking place—Collins English Dictionary's definition of broadcast being *to make widely known throughout an area*. This content belongs to, and is from, the organization releasing it. The platforms that we refer to as *social media* are being used to broadcast—*push*—that content onto the mobile devices of interested parties rather than those parties having to visit the organization or its website. I have no problem with this. It sounds eminently sensible. But it is not social media *marketing* in the sense of *engagement*. A school announcing a snow day on Instagram is not marketing. A police department announcing on Twitter that a road is closed after an accident is not marketing. A teacher giving formative feedback to homework questions on Facebook is not marketing.

Messages like this are dubbed social media *marketing* simply because an organization has published the information on a social media platform. Indeed, *any* content put on *any* social media platform by *any* organization, business, brand, establishment, entity, association, institute, society, corporation, company, alliance, union, enterprise (you get my drift) is considered to be social media *marketing*. It isn't. Yes, all of these bodies *could* use social media for marketing purposes—but giving out information on social media platforms is not social media marketing, it is communication.

But "hold on Alan" I hear some of you saying: "isn't a police department *communicating* that a road is closed after an accident part of the service they provide?" Well, yes—you would be right. I have already made it clear the *service* can be an objective for social media marketing. So if dissemination of information *is* marketing, and as it's on social media platforms, it must be social media marketing. Mustn't it?

---

[2] When you read this, the passing of time should have proved me right or wrong.

If we are to accept this as being the case, it removes a lot of the issues I have raised in this book, but invokes others. If your objective is to *engage* with customers you need the *right* culture, the *right* kind of C-level support, the *right* management and staff, and the *right* implementation. But if the message is information and its delivery is didactic, none of these is essential—or in some cases not even required. This brings us back to the 90-9-1 rule discussed in Chapter 2 (Section 2.1). Whilst much (all?) of the literature on social media marketing concentrates on *engagement*, what about that 90 percent who lurk but don't engage or contribute?

Could it be that they are simply reading the messages that are broadcast on those media we refer to as being *social*? Another spanner in the *engagement* works is research from Cebrian et al. (2017) which found that responses to social media events or stories were temporary and with regard to business, that "a new product, company, or service ... grabs people's attention for a single announcement and then flames out." This endorses social media being used for single, promotional, messages rather than the discussions or relationships that indicate *engagement*.

On the subject of engagement, I have long since put forward the notion that digital—and so by association, *social*—is actually causing customers (existing and potential) to *disengage* from organizations, brands, and products. Take, for example, comments made by Conrad Fritzsch, head of digital marketing at Mercedes-Benz, during a conference in Portugal in January 2017. He said that prior to the Internet, the average customer visited a dealer around nine times before buying a car. That is now down to an average of less than one and a half visits per purchase. I accept the fact that this may be lowering costs, but it is preventing any kind of real-life—that is; *not* virtual—relationship forming between seller and buyer. And if you are reading this book I am assuming you are business savvy enough to realize that the big money in being a car dealership is in after sales service, not the car's sale itself. Furthermore, this virtual relationship only exists if the buyer has used Internet platforms owned or controlled by Mercedes or the dealership. If this is not the case, then any relationship formed during the online Mercedes car-buying process is not made with the German auto maker but the organization, platform, or media that provided the information potential buyers sought in helping them down the sales funnel. Therefore, when the car needs servicing the owner is likely to refer to the source of information they found most useful. In other words, instead of instinctively contacting the seller with whom a relationship has been formed—in the *old* days, the dealership— they tweet or post "where's the best place to get my Merc serviced?"

An addendum to this section would be to enlarge on why I have this opinion on *disengagement*. The answer has its origins in comments I made in Chapter 5 (Section 5.1) where I make the point that digital marketing is *marketing*. Add into that my experience in sales and you have someone who has experience—and has seen the benefits of—developing genuine relationships with customers. By *genuine*, I mean face-to-face, how are the kids, let's chat a while over a coffee, get to know you *engagement*. Those customers come back for the car's service because of that relationship. Not because they got an e-mail or tweet. And guess what? When it's time to replace that car with another, they don't ask their *friends* on Facebook; they call at the dealership, have a chat over a cup of coffee and write a check for $70,000. I'll also remind you that in the same section of Chapter 5 (Section 5.1) I rail against digital gurus who know nothing about marketing. Well add to that: *and have no idea whatsoever how to sell anything to anyone*. The irony is that despite their dubious reputation in some quarters, the *best* car sales folk are some of the best sales folk; period. Therefore, they are ideally placed to recognize when their bosses have bought into the Emperor's New *Digital* Clothes.

It has long been my opinion that the vast majority of people who *friend*, *like* (or whatever) an organization, brand, or product on a social platform are either (a) already a customer, or (b) are never realistically going to be one. More recently however—prompted by the result of the UK's Brexit vote and the election of Donald Trump as president of the United States—interest has developed around the existence of so-called online *echo chambers*. For example, Alex Krasodomski-Jones (2017), a researcher at the Centre for the Analysis of Social Media, found that politically engaged Twitter users are more likely to interact with others who support the same party and share articles from publications that match their beliefs. Note that an earlier version of these chambers is *information bubbles*, where we stay within our own online bubble when assimilating information. This is a rather obvious extension of our offline behavior where we tend to spend most time with like-minded groups of people.

Such research is, of course, societal but my view on the issue stems from my knowledge and understanding of good old-fashioned marketing. More specifically, the model of *segmentation*. That is: the notion that a product will be purchased by like-minded folk thus making them a target group for marketing efforts. The trick is to identify and reach those target consumers. Traditionally, this is made easier if consumers identified themselves as users of the product by buying them. Then along came the Internet and you showed your allegiance by *liking* those organizations, brands, or products on a social platform. So, does being in the social media *club* increase your loyalty to the brand or product? Well, maybe—but if the product is right for you, and it sells at a price that is agreeable to you, and it is available in a place convenient to you, aren't you likely to repurchase without having clicked on a *like* button?

Note that it is this notion that only existing customers *like* organizations, brands, or products that is behind much of the research presented as *proving* that engagement increases sales. Such research—and I've seen quite a lot—states that customers who have *liked* or *follow* a commercial entity will spend *more* money with that organization, brand, or product than someone who has not *liked* or *followed* them. Hold that thought whilst considering the following scenario.

- Customer A has made a purchase with which they are happy—happy enough to seek out the relevant social media presence and express their satisfaction with a *like, follow,* or whatever.
- Customer B has made a purchase with which they are reasonably happy—but not so happy as to express their satisfaction on social media by *liking, following,* or whatever.
- Customer C has made a purchase which they consider to be OK, but not outstanding and they have not expressed that on social media by *liking, following,* or whatever.

The perceived wisdom of the followers-buy-more argument is that customer A will spend more than customers B or C. As this is not a strictly academic text, I'll use the not-academic comment of: *well duh*? I'll go even further by asking this question. Will customer A spend more money with the said organization, brand, or product *because* they have *liked* or *followed* them? Or will they spend more money with them because they provide the right product in the right place at the right price?

Meeting the needs and expectations of customers does not require social media. Not every organization, brand, or product has to have a dialog with customers to bring value to customers. That being *social* is not part of the corporate culture is not a precursor to lost customers and sales. Just ask Apple, they seem to be doing quite well despite having a Facebook presence that has no postings.

I have frequently heard or read comments something like: "marketers are well aware of the potential of social media to reach customers." The key word in this endorsement of social media marketing is *customers*. As in existing—not potential. People who join an organization, brand, or product on Facebook, Twitter, or any other platform do so because they have already been satisfied with a purchase—or maybe because they got the right product in the right place for the right price? Try reversing this notion. Would anyone *like* or *follow* a seller if they didn't provide them with the right product in the right place for the right price? Donald Trump's use of social media has been a reoccurring theme throughout this book, well consider this. His Tweets are designed to hit the mark with his supporters (i.e., target market), which they do extremely well. That others disagree with them is the essence of segmentation. Those who follow @therealdonaldtrump voted for him—they are *satisfied* with the product he offers.[3]

Furthermore, as the research presented in Chapter 2 (Section 2.4) suggests, a significant number of consumers join social media sites solely to find out about discounts and gain access to coupons. That's not social media marketing (i.e., *engaging with customers*) it's using social media platforms to distribute promotions. In these instances customers do not wish to *engage* with the organization, brand, or product—they just want to save money. Which is fine. But please, let's not have those organization's flaunt that they are actively *engaging* with their customer base on social media because they have a zillion *likes*. For those organizations, the

---

[3] I do appreciate that there will be a number of journalists and others who may follow this Twitter account in order to report on, or criticize the tweets without actually having voted for President Trump.

*likes* are the same as an e-mail list—but with a lower delivery and click-through rate. I wonder if any organization has done some kind of cost–benefit analysis of coupons physically delivered to people's homes against those placed on social media. Sure, the social media might be cheaper (*might*—it is not free), but if no one responds it is a waste of time. Plus, despite the technology, coupons in letter boxes can be targeted at local stores far more efficiently.

Furthermore, if we consider social media for carrying a marketing message, the findings of the Adobe Email Survey 2016, conducted by Adobe Digital Insights (ADI), make grim reading for sellers of the Emperor's New *Digital* Clothes. Respondents—which included an appropriate proportion of Millennials—were asked: "when it comes to receiving offers from marketers, how do you prefer to be contacted by brands." The answers are shown in Figure 7.1.

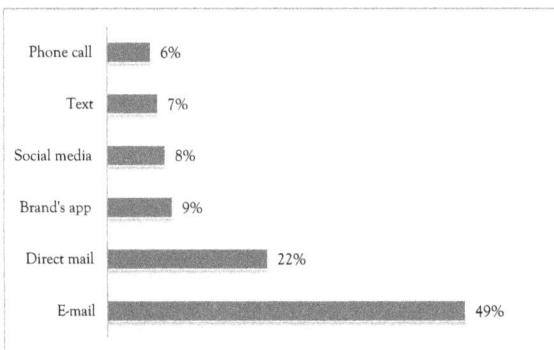

*Figure 7.1  Preferred method of hearing from brands*

Given that nearly three times as many people would rather receive a marketing message via good old-fashioned post than social media, perhaps I should have put this on page one and then skipped to the last chapter? I should also add that e-mail marketing has an established model for determining return on investment.

As detailed at the end of Chapter 2, there are also a significant number of *followers* of individuals (e.g., actors, musicians) or entities (e.g., movies, stage shows) that people *like* as a show of affinity to the brand that is that person or entity. Furthermore, as addressed in that chapter, those *likes* are frequently made to impress online *friends* and nothing more. Again, social media can be used to push messages out to fans, but there is little or no aspect of engagement.

Then there are the followers I rank as *never realistically going to be a customer*. There can be a number of reasons for this, but I would suggest it is because they fall into one of two groups:

1. Me-too followers—these people notice that their friends *(real or virtual)* like a product or service and so they click the *like/follow* button as well. The story of the vegetarian sandwich seller in Chapter 4 (Section 4.4) where the majority of followers were not geographically close enough to *realistically* be customers is an example of this.
2. Window shoppers or dreamers. For example, on the day I wrote this, the Ferrari official Facebook Page had 16,432,443 likes. Yes, I do appreciate how branding works, but really, how many of those people is, or are ever likely to be, a buyer of a $150,000 plus super car? They might buy a Ferrari baseball cap or tee shirt, but that is more akin to a *like* on Facebook than it is a purchase of the brand. I'll even give you an argument that many Ferrari owners either do not wish others to know they are part of the brand's *scuderia*, or are not social media aficionados. The reverse, of course, can apply. I'm sure if a member of the Kardashian family bought a new Ferrari the social world would know about it long before its tyres touched the tarmac, but such folk are in the minority.

So the book's titular question remains. For some organizations, brands, and products social media marketing *is* a marketing panacea. For others, managers have fallen hook, line, and sinker for the Emperor's New *Digital* Clothes, and social media marketing is not suitable for them. But we also have a third group. They have bought the Emperor's New *Digital* Clothes, but because of their unsuitability to use social media for *engagement* they have stumbled on a different, but effective, use of social media platforms.

You will recall Zhu and Chen's social media matrix from Chapter 2, where the various uses of social media are split into those that address content- and profile-based against customized and broadcast messages (see Table 2.1). However, as we near the end of this voyage on the stormy seas that are social media and the marketing efforts that

**Table 7.1 The social media marketing mix (adopted from Zhu and Chen 2015)**

|  | Customized message | Broadcast message |
|---|---|---|
| **Profile-based** | **Relationship** <br> Allows marketers to connect, communicate, and build relationships. | **Self-Media** <br> Allows marketers to broadcast their messages and for and others to follow. |
| **Content-based** | **Collaboration** <br> Allows marketers to provide answers, advice, and help. | **Creative outlet** <br> Allows marketers to share their products with potential customers. |

set sail on it, it is useful to adapt this matrix for social media marketers to identify what the aims of their social media presence might be (see Table 7.1).

In this *marketing* version of Zhu and Chen's social media mix the platform examples for each quadrant are removed. This is because the same platforms might be equally suitable for multiple aims—although the content and its tone would need to be significantly different, Twitter, for example, could be used for:

- Collaboration: an after-sales service as per many airlines and service providers
- Self-media: how Donald Trump and other celebrities use Twitter
- Creative outlet: product promotion as per clothes retailers
- Relationship: communicating with customers and non-customers as *friends* as per so many examples given in the previous chapter.

Relationship is deliberately placed at the end of this list. This is because *relationship* is perceived as *being* the essence of what *social media* marketing is. But we have moved on. It is no longer compulsory for the various platforms we label as being *social* media to be *social*. They are media. Furthermore, they are media platforms on which marketing messages can be delivered. Which leads us to a social media eureka moment:

Social media marketing is about *engagement*

Anything else is marketing *on* social media

Once we accept this, it changes the answer to this book's titular question. Indeed, this means the social media marketing mix could be revised to incorporate this aspect (see Table 7.2).

You will recall how in so many of the failed social media marketing examples in the previous chapter the practitioners have treated *collaboration*, *self-media*, and *creative outlet* as relationship tools rather than marketing tools. If these three options have been—mistakenly—used to be *social* (i.e., building relationships) with customers then the Emperor's New *Digital* Clothes analogy is proved in that managers have blindly adopted a me-too strategy.

Furthermore, you will recall that in Chapter 4 (Section 4.3) return on investment was considered. The results weren't very favorable—but one of the key issues was that marketers are struggling to measure the return

*Table 7.2  Marketing on social media*

|  | Customized message | Broadcast message |
|---|---|---|
| **Profile-based** | **Relationship** (social media marketing) Allows marketers to connect, communicate, and build relationships with social media messages that are not *promotional* in nature. | **Self-Media** (marketing on social media) Allows marketers to broadcast their promotional messages (e.g., discount offers) to followers (existing customers) as social media content that can be acted upon, liked, followed, and forwarded by the target audience. |
| **Content-based** | **Service** (marketing on social media) Allows marketers to provide answers, advice, and help, most commonly as a form of after-sales or customer support service. | **Creative outlet** (advertising on social media) Allows marketers to share their product and brand information—including promotions—with a wider audience of potential customers using programmatic advertising that targets user data. |

on any investment in social media marketing. That would be, of course, measurement of *social* engagement. Naturally, that remains a problem for any *true* social media marketing—but for marketing on social media, three of the four quadrants can use metrics that are more traditional in nature. A "10% off this product for the next 7 days" tweet can be measured in the similar fashion as the same message placed in a newspaper or radio ad, for example. Could it be, however, that some social media marketing evangelists wouldn't be too keen on this? Could it be that the results would see those budgets move back to *traditional* marketing—with none going to improve the Emperor's new wardrobe? Perish the thought.

Of course, *relationship* does work for *some* organizations, brands, and products and that is where the whole issue of culture is so relevant. If you do have the right culture you can (or might) be successful in using *collaboration*, *self-media*, and *creative outlet* as part of developing a relationship with consumers. You *might* even be able to use the same content and tone of voice in all four elements of the matrix. But—and it is a big *but*—that only works for those organizations, brands, and products that are *social* by nature and/or are *right* for social media marketing. And I think that is less than 5 percent of all organizations, brands, or products in the world. For the other 95 percent: welcome to the Emperor's New *Digital* Clothes.

That 95 percent should not despair, however. To ignore social media as *media* for getting across a marketing message to a targeted audience—*marketing on social media*—would be to throw out the baby with the bathwater. That said, I am still convinced that for *some* organizations, *some* brands, and *some* products the use of any social media for any kind of marketing message is not a viable option. And I think that could represent a significant percentage of all organizations, brands, and products. I say this because there are just *so* many businesses, not-for-profit and public sector organizations out there. If you are now shouting at the book in disgust—and there should be some, otherwise there never were any Emperor's New *Digital* Clothes—I refer you to Chapter 6 (Section 6.1) where I listed products I purchased over a week or so for which social media marketing (that is: *marketing on social media*) was not only unsuitable, but not required. I'll go further and say that many businesses do not need to do *any* promotional activity. If they provide the *right* product in the *right* place and the *right* price they can sustain a healthy profit based purely on repeat purchase and word-of-mouth referrals. Doubt that? Try; my electrician, my financial adviser, my plumber, my local gas station, my local greengrocer, my local post office, my window cleaner, and just about every local retailer in my town's shopping center—along with all of those *everything's a pound* outlets (that's a *dollar* in your town). If they don't need to conduct any promotional activities they most certainly don't need to do any social media marketing.

To use *any* social media platform for *any* form of marketing when it is—for *any* reason—unsuitable simply because others are doing so is not good practice. To use *any* social media platform for *any* form of marketing because someone tells you it is a good idea means you have been taken in by the Emperor's New *Digital* Clothes.

Which brings us around to a principal of effective marketing. There is never a single *right* solution that suits *every* organization, *every* brand, or *every* product in *every* scenario in *every* location *all* of the time. Ultimately, therefore, the answer to the question of whether social media marketing is a marketing panacea or an example of the Emperor's New *Digital* Clothes is the same answer to the question of whether *any* element of marketing is *right* for an organization, brand, or product; *it depends*.

It depends on the organization.
It depends on the product.
It depends on the brand.
It depends on the time.
It depends on the place.

It depends on whether or not it is *right* for the organization, brand, or product. And that is why marketing just isn't as easy as some folks would have you believe.

# References

Anderson, C. 2006. *The Long Tail*. Hyperion Books.

Arndt, J. 1967. *Word of Mouth Advertising: A Review of the Literature*. New York: Advertising Research Foundation.

Bagozzi, R.P., and U.M. Dholakia. 2006. "Antecedents and Purchase Consequences of Customer Participation in Small Group Brand Communities." *International Journal of Research in Marketing* 23, no. 1, pp. 45–61.

Barnes, N.G., and C. Daubitz. 2017. *Time for Re-evaluation? Social Media and the 2016 Inc. 500*. Center for Marketing Research, University of Massachusetts, available online at http://www.umassd.edu/cmr/socialmedia-research/2017inc500/

Battelle, J. 2005. *Search*. Nicholas Brealey Publishing.

Blau, P.M. 1964. *Exchange and Power in Social Life*. New York: Wiley.

Brodie, R.J., L.D. Hollebeek, B. Juric, and A. Ilic. 2013. "Consumer Engagement in a Virtual Brand Community: An Exploratory Analysis." *Journal of Business Research* 66, no. 1, pp. 105–14.

Brown, D., and S. Fiorella. 2013. *Influence Marketing*. Que Publishing.

Cebrian, M., I. Rahwan, and A. Pentland. 2017. "Beyond Viral: Generating Sustainable Value from Social Media." *MIT Sloan Management Review*, available at sloanreview.mit.edu/article/beyond-viral-generating-sustainable-value-from-social-media/

Charlesworth, A. 2007. *Key Concepts in e-Commerce*. Palgrave MacMillan.

Charlesworth, A. 2009. *Internet Marketing—Practical Approach*. Butterworth Heinman.

Charlesworth, A. 2014. *Digital Marketing—a Practical Approach*. 2nd ed. Routledge.

Charlesworth, A. 2015. *An Introduction to Social Media Marketing*. Routledge.

Childnet International 2008. *"Young People and Social Networking Services."* A Childnet International Research Report, available at www.digizen.org/socialnetworking/downloads/Young_People_and_Social_Networking_Services_full_report.pdf

Cialdini, R. 1983. *Influence: The Psychology of Persuasion*. HarperBusiness.

CMO Survey 2016. *Social Media Spending Triples But Falls Short of Expectations*, available online at https://cmosurvey.org/blog/social-media-spending-triples-falls-short-expectations/

CMO Survey 2017. *Highlights and Insights*, available online at https://cmosurvey.org/wp-content/uploads/sites/11/2016/08/The_CMO_Survey-Highlights_and_Insights-Aug-2016.pdf

Cohen, H. 2010. *Old Spice's Viral Social Media Drives Sales*, available online at www.heidicohen.com/old-spice's-viral-social-media-drives-sales

Dixon, M., and L. Ponomareff. 2010. *Why Your Customers Don't Want to Talk to You*. Havard Business Review.

Eisenberg, B. 2008. *Understanding and Aligning the Values of Social media*. FutureNow.

First Direct 2013. *The "Ranters" and "Peacocks"—New Personality Types in Social Media Revealed*. Press release, April 10, 2013.

Frenzen, J., and K. Nakamoto. 1993. "Structure, Cooperation and the Flow of Market Information." *Journal of Consumer Research* 20, no. 3, pp. 360–75.

Fry, S. 2016. "Too Many People Have Peed in the Pool." *The Old Friary blog*, available at www.stephenfry.com/2016/02/peedinthepool/

Godin, S. 2007. Meatball Sundae. Piatkus.

Granovetter, M. 1973. "The Strength of Weak Ties." *American Journal of Sociology* 78, no. 6, pp. 1360–80.

Greenwood, S., A. Perrin, and M. Duggan. 2016. *The Social Media Matrix*. Pew Research Center, available online at www.pewinternet.org/2016/11/11/social-media-update-2016-methodology/

Hammersley, M., and P. Atkinson. 1997. *Ethnography: Principles in Practice*. 2nd ed. Routledge.

Homans, G.C. 1958. "Social Behaviour as Exchange." *American Journal of Sociology* 63, no. 6, pp. 597–606.

Homans, G.C. 1961. *Social Behaviour: Its Elementary Forms*. New York: Harcourt, Brace & World, Inc.

John, L.K., D. Mochon, O. Emrich, and J. Schwartz. 2017. *What's the Value of a Like?* Harvard Business Review, March–April 2017 Issue, available online at https://hbr.org/2017/03/whats-the-value-of-a-like

Kabani, S. 2013. *The Zen of Social Media Marketing: An Easier Way to Build Credibility, Generate Buzz, and Increase Revenue*. 3rd ed. BenBella Books.

Kamal, I. 2011. The Social Media Measurement Imperative: Building Business Value, available online at www.emarketer.com/Article/Social-Media-Measurement-Imperative-Building-Business-Value/1008727

Kaplan, A.M., and M. Haenlein. 2010. "Users of the World, Unite! The Challenges and Opportunities of Social Media." *Business Horizons* 53, no. 1, pp. 59–68.

Katz, E., and P.F. Lazarsfeld. 1955. *Personal Influence: The Part Played by People in the Flow of Mass Communications*. The Free Press.

Keen, A. 2007. *The Cult of the Amateur: How Today's Internet is Killing our Culture*. New York: Doubleday/Random House.

Kozinets, R. 1997. "I Want To Believe: A Netnography of The X-Philes' Subculture of Consumption." *Advances in Consumer Research* 24, pp. 470–75.

L2 2017. Intelligence Report: Social Platforms 2017. www.L2inc.com

Krasodomski-Jones, A. 2017. *Talking to Ourselves.* Centre for the Analysis of Social Media. available at www.demos.co.uk/project/talking-to-ourselves/

Kumar, A., R. Bezawada, R. Rishika, R. Janakiraman, and P.K. Kannan. 2016. "From Social to Sale: The Effects of Firm-Generated Content in Social Media on Customer Behavior." *Journal of Marketing* 80, pp. 7–25.

Levine, R., C. Locke, D. Searls, and D. Weinberger. 1999. *The Cluetrain Manifesto: The End of Business as Usual.* Basic Books.

Markerly, Inc. 2016. *Instagram Marketing: Does Influencer Size Matter?* Featured article, available at www.markerly.com/blog/instagram-marketing-does-influencer-size-matter/

McCain, J.L., and W.K. Campbell. 2016. *Narcissism and Social Media Use: A Meta-Analytic Review.* Psychology of Popular Media Culture, November 10, 2016.

McConnell, B., and J. Huba. 2007. *Citizen Marketers.* Kaplan.

McDonald, M., P. Mouncey, and S. Maklan. 2014. *Marketing Value Metrics.* Kogan Page.

Mullally, J., and A. Lalji. 2016. *About Face.* BBDO Worldwide, available online at wiredrive.bbdo.com/facebook/AboutFace-ANewApproachtoFacebookforBigBrands.pdf

Nielsen, J. October 9, 2006. *Participation Inequality: Encouraging More Users to Contribute.* Alertbox. Message posted to www.useit.com/alertbox/participation_inequality.html

Owen, P., and C. Wright. 2009. Our Top 10 Funniest YouTube Comments—What are Yours? *The Guardian.* London, available at www.theguardian.com/technology/blog/2009/nov/03/youtube-funniest-comments

Pew Research Center 2016. *Online Shopping and E-Commerce,* available online at assets.pewresearch.org/wp-content/uploads/sites/14/2016/12/16113209/PI_2016.12.19_Online-Shopping_FINAL.pdf

Pew Research Center 2017. Global Attitudes Survey 2016, available online at http://pewresearch.org/fact-tank/2017/04/20/not-everyone-in-advanced-economies-is-using-social-media/

Pipeline Marketing 2016. The State of Pipeline Marketing Report, available online at http://www.pipelinemarketing.com/

PiperJaffray 2016. *Taking Stock With Teens, Fall 2016.* Press release, available online at www.piperjaffray.com/2col.aspx

Reichelt, J., J. Sievert, and F. Jacob. 2014. "How Credibility Affects eWOM Reading: The Influences of Expertise, Trustworthiness, and Similarity on Utilitarian and Social Functions." *Journal of Marketing Communications* 20, nos. 1–2, pp. 65–81.

Rogers, E. 1962. *Diffusion of Innovations.* Free Press.

Roy, A. 2014. *Influencer Marketing Status.* Augure. No longer available.

Sign-Up Technologies Ltd 2013. Twitter Marketing: What Results Should You Expect? available on www.signupto.com/news/permission-marketing/twitter-marketing-what-results-should-you-expect-infographic/

SimplyMeasured State of Social Marketing Annual Report 2016, available online at https://simplymeasured.com/blog/introducing-the-2016-state-of-social-marketing-report

SimplyMeasured State of Social Marketing Annual Report 2017, available online at https://get.simplymeasured.com/2017-07-12-State-of-Social-em.html

SocialChorus Platform 2014. "Tips for Working with Blogger Advocates." *SocialChorus Blog,* available online at www.socialchorus.com/blogger-advocate-landscape-tips-tricks-working-different-blogger-verticals-infographic

Sprout Social 2015. Q4 2015 Sprout Social Index. SproutSocial.com, available on www.sproutsocial.com/insights/data/the-sprout-social-index-q4-2015/

Sprout Social 2016. Q3 2016 Sprout Social index. SproutSocial.com, available on www.sproutsocial.com/insights/data/q3-2016

Sprout Social 2017. Q1 2017 Sprout Social index, available on www.sproutsocial.com/insights/data/q1-2017/

Standage, T. 2013. *Writing on the Wall.* Bloomsbury.

SUMO Heavy Industries 2016. *Social Commerce Survey; The Future of eCommerce?* available on info.sumoheavy.com/2016/

Tapscott, D., and A.D. Williams. 2006. *Wikinomics.* Portfolio.

Technorati Media 2013. *Digital Influence Report,* available online at www.technorati.com/report/2013-dir/

Thibaut, J.W., and H.H. Kelley. 1959. *The Social Psychology of Groups.* New York: John Wiley and Sons.

Weber, L. 2007. *Marketing to the Social Web.* Wiley.

Weil, D. 2009. *The Corporate Blogging Book.* Piatkus Books.

Zhu, Y.-Q., and H.-G. Chen. 2015. "Social Media and Human Need Satisfaction: Implications for Social Media Marketing." *Business Horizons* 58, no. 3, pp. 335–45.

# Index

www.ingramcontent.com/pod-product-compliance
Lightning Source LLC
Chambersburg PA
CBHW060611210326
41519CB00014B/3632